Erin Shale is a careers guidance cou at Balwyn High School and has teacher and counsellor for many yea has written a number of successful for parents and teenagers, including *Adolescence: A guide for parents* with Michael Carr-Gregg and *The Complete Survival Guide for High School and Beyond*, and edited the anthology *Inside Out*.

'An ideal antidote for any anxious parent of a teenager—full of humour, commonsense and sound practical advice.'
—*Ian Renard, Chancellor, University of Melbourne (and father of four daughters)*

'As a psychologist working in schools and as a parent, I will be using this book both personally and professionally, and will be recommending it to friends, colleagues and clients as a positive way to decode the often secret parent business, and to enable parents to support their teenagers at school. Parents don't have to learn from their mistakes, but by reading this book!'
—*Sandra Groves, educational psychologist*

'I cannot say how much I enjoyed this book—for its commonsense, or rather, its wisdom, based on much experience and wide reading; for its generous and skilful use of quotation from students, parents and teachers; for its clear and vigorous style and for its flashes of humour.

This is a book I would like to give to every parent and every student. It knows all the sorts of problems they face, and all the usually wrong reactions and all the right approaches.'
—*Emeritus Professor Richard Johnson, Visiting Fellow, Centre for Academic Development and Educational Method, Australian National University*

'I've been an educator for more than 30 years, I've been a parent for more than 20 years and I've asked just about every one of the questions in this book! ... This book provides a series of topics and explanations about school, young people and the world that all parents and teachers will find informative, fun and revealing.'
—*Associate Professor Stephen Crump, Faculty of Education, University of Sydney*

'As a parent I know that we all wonder what we can do to ensure our children make the most of their schooling, both socially and academically. *How's school?* is a useful and practical guide for parents, carers, grandparents, teachers and health providers as they help young people develop the skills, attitudes and attributes to navigate their way successfully through their schooling and help to prepare them for the world outside of school.

I encourage all parents and others interested in supporting young people through their schooling to read this excellent book.'
—*The Hon Dr Brendan Nelson MP, Minister for Education, Science and Training*

'Erin Shale has combined her extensive knowledge of young people, born from her experience as a counsellor and teacher in secondary schools, with a deep professional expertise in her field.

This book will be a valued guide to parents with teenagers. Help is at hand! It provides a ray of hope and wise advice on the many thorny issues that confront families . . .'
—*E.J. Brierley, President, Australian Secondary Principals Association*

'In this guide for parents of teenagers, Erin Shale shares the practical wisdom and insight gained from her many years of counselling teenagers and their parents . . .

The special and welcome focus of her work is on the relationship between parenting and schooling. This book has many, many suggestions and practical illustrations on how we as parents can provide positive support for our children through the years of secondary schooling . . .'
—*Josephine Lonergan AM, Executive Director, Australian Parents Council*

Erin Shale

How's School?

Helping your teenager
get the most
out of high school

ALLEN&UNWIN

First published in 2005

Allen & Unwin
83 Alexander Street
Crows Nest NSW 2065
Australia
Phone: (61 2) 8425 0100
Fax: (61 2) 9906 2218
Email: info@allenandunwin.com
Web: www.allenandunwin.com

National Library of Australia
Cataloguing-in-Publication entry:

Shale, Erin.
How's school?: helping your teenager get the most out of school.

Includes index.
ISBN 1 74114 669 0.

1. High school students—Australia—Handbooks, manuals, etc. 2. Education—
Parent participation—Handbooks, manuals, etc. 3. Student aspirations—
Australia—Handbooks, manuals, etc. I. title.

373.18

Set in 11/14 pt Legacy Serif Book by Midland Typesetters, Victoria, Australia
Printed by Griffin Press, South Australia

10 9 8 7 6 5 4 3 2 1

Contents

For my parents Marji and Peter Shale
who encouraged me to love learning
and to believe that nothing is impossible.

Acknowledgements

I am very grateful to all those who so generously shared their experiences with me and allowed me to quote them in this book.

I owe a special debt of gratitude to Jackie Yowell, who advised and supported me while I was researching this book. I treasure the conversations we shared, which helped shape my thoughts and writings into a possible book. I am also extremely fortunate to have had the support of the wonderful staff at Allen & Unwin. Their dedication and professionalism made my work as a writer immeasurably more enjoyable. In particular, special thanks to Elizabeth Weiss, Karen Gee and Catherine Taylor.

How's School? could not have been written without the continued support and interest my family have shown in my career and my writing. And last (but certainly not least) I acknowledge a special thank you to Nancy Huang who offered me just the right mix of insightful feedback, encouragement and a critical eye when I most needed it.

Introduction

Who can forget their school days? Some of us have fond memories, while others recall the whole experience with simmering resentment. Either way, there's no denying that the high school years are an indelible part of our childhood and have a huge influence on our life.

As a high school teacher and careers counsellor, working in schools day after day, I am still struck by how diverse young people are. Some leave high school brimming with confidence, heads held high, looking life square in the eyes. Others leave looking pretty much as they did when they first entered, somewhat bewildered and still wondering what the point of the whole thing has been. What amazes me is the transformation some students are able to achieve—like the shy kid who becomes a champion debater, or the antisocial rebel who ends up school captain.

If the schoolyard and the classroom are indeed the training grounds for life, it is crucial that we give young people the best possible start so they leave school well equipped to thrive in the wider world. School is more than a place where children acquire facts and knowledge. It is also where they learn to step outside the family setting, successfully interact with others and acquire life skills. In essence, it is a training ground for effective interpersonal relations and the self-esteem and self-acceptance needed to bounce back from life's knocks and make the most of life's opportunities.

So how's your son or daughter doing at school? When you ask that all-important question, 'How's school?', what answers do you get? What lies behind the grunt or flippant 'Okay'?

I have known many parents of schoolchildren, and without exception they wanted the best for their children, although many agonised over how education could best provide this. Many parents make sacrifices to give their children opportunities they never had themselves—the violin lessons, self-defence classes, extra tutoring. Some parents move to a new home to get a child into a particular school; some even leave countries they love in order to make a better life for their children.

As a parent, despite all your hard work and sacrifices, you still worry. It comes with the territory. 'Will they do well?' parents ask themselves. 'Are they making friends? What should I do to help them do better? Am I saying the right things? Should I do things differently? What can I do to help them get more out of school?' This is where this book comes in. In a nutshell, it's all about how you can help your child to make the schooling experience more fulfilling—academically, socially and emotionally. It doesn't matter whether you are a traditional mum-and-dad combo, stepparents, a single parent, guardian, grandparent or gay couple: anyone raising teenagers during the high school years faces similar issues. For economy of expression, I'll use the term 'parent' to cover all possibilities.

This book differs from other parenting books in its specific focus on the relationship between parenting and schooling. Let's face it: young people spend more than half their waking hours in school and school-related activities, so it stands to reason that teenage development is greatly influenced by experiences at school.

School—like home—should be a safe place where young people can learn the skills and values they need, not simply to survive but to thrive in the world beyond the school gates. Research shows that teenagers who feel a connectedness to home and school are more likely to be happy and resilient, and less likely to engage in negative pursuits.[1] For unhappy teenagers, the high school years can seem an eternity. If schooling is a positive experience, through which teenagers develop self-worth and identity, they can deal with the difficult self-questioning involved in leaving childhood and entering the unknown territory of adulthood.

I decided to write this book because of the countless parents who have approached me for advice. I hope to bring my twenty-odd years' experience from the other side of the desk to share with you some stories and insights. I've had so many sessions with parents and teenagers—together, separately, in laughter and in tears. I've heard both sides of the story. While there are many issues, I can assure you no student is beyond rescue, no crisis irresolvable. I have liberally sprinkled the text with FAQs (frequently asked questions) that echo through my many years of teaching and counselling.

I hope they will help answer yours as they arise during the challenging and exciting years your teenager will experience at high school.

Knowledge is power. Parents know their children better than anyone else and remain the most important people in their lives (but don't hold your breath waiting for them to tell you this). What I can offer you, however, is a professional, impartial view about helping teenagers find school more fulfilling, so they may develop into happier, more successful and confident young adults. My work gives me invaluable insights into how to best approach the good and the bad, the ugly and the beautiful scenarios that unfold as your child moves through high school.

Having a good understanding of the special skills your son or daughter needs to do well at high school will enable you to take a positive role in these vital life-shaping years. Next time you ask, 'So how's school?' you'll be able to greet your child's response in a way that will help them feel valued, supported and ready to face the next day with renewed confidence and optimism.

Part I
PARENT POWER
what you can do

1

How to help your teenager at school

Children are the sum of what parents contributed to their lives.

—Richard L. Strauss

Parent power is that extraordinary potential you have to influence and shape your children's attitudes, outlook on life and, most significantly, their ability to accept and feel good about themselves. After all, those who raise children are the most significant influence in their lives.

'What power?' I hear you say. 'I can't even get them to turn off the TV!' True, there is that small hitch called teenage rebellion, when your influence has diminished and all that matters to teenagers is what their friends do or think. It's just the natural breaking-away process teenagers go through. Of course they'll develop opinions and interests of their own and often challenge your view of the world. But be assured that behind that mask of 'I-know-it-all' bravado is a child who needs and longs for your acceptance and affirmation.

Parent power is an ever-present force, an invisible thread connecting parents and children. With a word, a look, a touch, you have the power to build up your children or tear them down, to make them feel accepted or rejected. Used negatively, parent power can strangle and deeply wound. Used well, it can centre them and allow them to step out confidently into the world, secure that they won't lose their moorings and spin out into space. How often do you think about your own childhood, and what your parents said or did not say, which crushed you or made you feel on top of the world?

Parents are the cornerstones of our identity. Not surprisingly, many adults publicly thank their parents at significant moments in their lives. Nicole Kidman thanked her mother when she received her Best Actress Oscar. She spoke of always wanting to make her mother proud, saying this had been a driving force for her entire life. It's so true that we need the acceptance and approval of our parents. Do your children know you're proud of them? Do they know they are the cornerstones of your life too?

You are the first mirror your teenager holds up in order to see their image. The affirmation, praise and encouragement you give determine whether they see a positive or negative picture. Throughout their lives, they see this reflection as they seek to work out who they are and whether they like this person.

Never under-estimate what you can do as a parent. If you don't accept your teenagers and offer them respect and dignity, they may spend the rest of their lives trying to exorcise the hurt, disappointment and even the anger this can cause. Your unconditional love and support, regardless of the paths they choose, will equip them to face school and life as confident, self-assured and happy young adults.

Parent power—that awesome ability to affect and shape the life of your child—is in your hands. Use it well!

How does parent power apply to school? Whether your child is about to leave primary school, or is already in high school, you can adopt strategies to enhance their experiences of school. Whether they love, hate, are relaxed at or indifferent to school, you can help them maximise their potential in all areas of school life: their work, their social life and their inner life. Myriad factors play a part in this, but the greatest influence comes from parents.

Before investigating strategies parents can use to support teenagers through high school, let's look at the ingredients teenagers need to make school a positive and affirming experience.

Ingredients of success: what your kids need

I've lost count of the number of parents who have told me they would do anything, pay anything, sacrifice anything to help their child be happier and do better at school. Comments parents read in reports are often frustrating. 'With a more consistent effort, Suzie could greatly improve her results in this subject.' 'Jack is not working to the best of his ability in this class. He is capable of much better work.' 'Emma is a talented student who needs only to participate in class and complete her work with more care in order to produce more pleasing results.'

Why do some students fly through school while others seem to crawl? What's really happening to the Suzies, Jacks and Emmas? Many people wrongly assume it all comes down to how 'bright' the student is. Academic success is *not* merely due to cognitive ability. Often the students who excel at school are no more gifted than those who drift along or even bomb out. Students who enjoy success and find school fulfilling simply have the right set of skills. They have what we'll refer to here as SAAS (skills, attitudes and attributes for success).

SAAS—Skills, attitudes and attributes for success

There are three groups of skills under the SAAS banner, including: personal skills; study and school skills; social and interpersonal skills.

Personal skills

- confidence;
- resilience;
- high self-esteem;
- optimism;
- determination;
- ability to handle stress;
- ability to empathise;
- sense of humour;
- openness to new challenges.

Study and school skills

- ability to balance study and other interests;
- ability to understand and utilise various learning styles;
- ability to organise and handle homework demands;
- good study technique;
- good exam technique;
- ability to set goals and to work to achieve them;

- good organisational skills;
- good time-management skills;
- good memory techniques;
- ability to speak well in public.

Social and interpersonal skills

- good communication skills;
- ability to work well and play well with others—to show and earn respect;
- ability to accept direction and criticism;
- ability to respond well in social situations—to possess charm;
- conflict management ability;
- ability to form positive friendships/relationships;
- problem-solving ability;
- decision-making ability;
- leadership ability.

Once you understand SAAS well, you'll be able to ascertain which skills and abilities your teenager already has and which can be improved upon. In Chapters 5 and 6 we'll examine these important skills in detail and outline practical strategies to help teenagers improve their competency in each. It makes sense that the more you know your teenager, the more you can help them.

How to know your teenager better

You probably know your teenager's best subjects and favourite sport. You might even know their interests and taste in music (even if it drives you nuts). But what are their strengths and limitations? What are their hopes and fears? What are their secret ambitions?

It takes time and effort to know someone, and your own children are no exception. Avoid the mistaken belief that, because you are their parents, you inherently know them well. You may think you and your children know all about each other, but you'd be surprised what I've heard when I ask: 'What does your father do?' Common answers are: 'He does something in business' or 'He works in an office.' Some go as far as to say 'No idea.' If this is how much they know about you, how much do you really know about them? Do you know what they do after school and where they go on weekends, for example?

Spare a moment now and take an honest look at your teenager. Looking critically at someone you love can be quite confronting, but it's also where you need to start when assessing their SAAS needs. Below are some suggestions to help you gain a better understanding of your teenager.

Make time to be with your teenager

Close interaction, sharing experiences, talking things over and sharing jokes are all needed to develop the bond between parents and children. Spending regular time with your teenager is a great way to gain insights into their strengths and skills.

Points to watch include:
◎ Can they confidently express an opinion?
◎ Do they acknowledge and accept other viewpoints?
◎ How do they react to setbacks? Are they resilient?
◎ Are they determined or do they give up easily?
◎ Can they accept criticism, follow directions and show evidence of problem-solving ability?
◎ Do they find it difficult to discuss problems?

Make time to know your teenager *now*. These years fly past and with them the opportunities to help teenagers build their character, resilience and self-identity. When your young adult emerges safely at the other end—and, miracle of miracles, you've survived too—you'll also have the satisfaction of knowing you helped them make the most of these formative years.

Be there, especially when they need you

You learn a lot about teenagers by being around at the important times in their lives. Watch them play sport and you'll see their competitive nature and good sportsmanship, or you may notice that they are uncomfortable around sports events. Attend the concert your teenager is in and you'll see them in a different light—perhaps this creative group activity suits them better. Go rock climbing with them and you may glimpse a different person again, one who thrives when they can set their own goals. Notice what your teenager avoids and what motivates them. There are few things more satisfying than seeing teenagers in their element, lost in the exhilaration of the moment. This is what matters, not how skilled they are at an activity.

Points to watch include:

- Does your teenager enjoy working in a team or alone?
- Do they relate well to peers?
- Are they competitive, or happier in a self-paced situation?
- Are they outgoing or reserved?
- Do they enjoy responsibility?
- Do they shine in, or shy away from, leadership roles?

Notice and share the fun times

You can understand teenagers more by observing them when they socialise with other people. Make their friends welcome in your home and you'll learn a lot from the relationship dynamics. And if you're lucky enough to be able to share an interest with your teenager, like the Grand Prix or science fiction movies, you're in another unique position to learn more about them.

Points to watch include:

- Does your teenager interact comfortably with others?
- Do they display empathy for others?
- How do they react when meeting new people? Are they confident or shy?
- Do they avoid situations where meeting new people is involved?
- Do they have a sense of humour?
- Are they happy for you to meet their friends?

Outside opinions

Talk to people who see your teenager in other situations. They can provide objective perceptions of your teenager and offer invaluable insights you may otherwise miss in your own interaction with your teen.

Other parents

You might not know the parents of all of your teenager's friends, but it's a good idea to know parents of their best friends. They may be able to share insights into aspects of your teenager you haven't seen. 'Karl is a lovely boy. He's been such a great help to Alan. He's been helping him catch up with his work since he broke his arm.' Or, 'Robyn has a terrific sense of humour. She keeps us laughing for hours.'

Teachers

Teachers see teenagers work and interact socially with peers, and often see personal qualities or insecurities parents are unaware of. At parent-teacher nights, don't only discuss results. Take the initiative and ask teachers whether your teenager seems happy at school. Do they enjoy class participation and have good interpersonal skills, or do they have difficulty interacting with others? Informal times such as sports days are also good opportunities to chat to teachers.

School reports

Read between the lines. School reports often indicate a teenager's strengths and limitations. The comment is as important as the score. 'Kelly could improve her work with a more positive attitude in class. She tends to allow herself to become distracted and sometimes distracts others. She must follow instructions.' Kelly probably isn't the most popular student with this teacher. Are other teachers making similar observations? Discover what is going on. Is Kelly's 'I don't care' attitude part of a rebellious stage where all adults are challenged, or is she having too much fun with friends in class to concentrate on her work? Is she hiding a learning difficulty? Consider all possibilities and discuss these with teachers to discover how you can best help your teenager.

The influence of parental hopes and dreams

Understanding your teenager's strengths and limitations is essential knowledge if you are to guide them. But you also need to acknowledge your own emotions and expectations of them. Parental hopes and dreams can lift and support teenagers or weigh them down. Acknowledge your hopes and dreams in case you push your teenager, even unconsciously, in these directions and their happiness is sacrificed.

The most common types of expectation causing parent-teenager tensions revolve around results and careers.

Results

Parents want to encourage teenagers to do well at school, but good intentions can sometimes cause more harm than good. There's a fine line between encouragement and pressure, and teenagers can also misconstrue parents' well-intentioned remarks.

Some parents who were good at school themselves naturally expect their teen to top the class in various subjects. Some parents have sacrificed much to provide for their kids and expect a reasonable 'return on investment' (I once heard a mother complaining that her daughter had given her a shocking return on investment after four years of private schooling).

Fair or not, we are all blessed with different abilities and qualities. Understand and accept your child's abilities so you can give them positive motivation rather than pressuring them to perform beyond their limits. The consequences of putting too much pressure on teenagers can be devastating. I see it all the time. 'Dad doesn't understand the meaning of the word "failure". He's always been good at everything and he expects us to be the same. It stresses me out because I'll never get the marks he wants.' Some students are so worried about disappointing their parents that their results decline under the strain. In extreme cases, students can resort to cheating in order to fulfill parental expectations or give up completely, fearing that they can only disappoint. Teenagers must understand that parental love and approval aren't riding on their results—that, regardless of what the next report contains, they don't have to be afraid of bringing it home.

Interests/choices/careers

Your teenagers may not remotely resemble the children of your dreams. The subjects they enjoy and the career direction they're investigating may surprise or even bewilder you. You adore classical music and history while they're completely engrossed in motorcycles and heavy metal music, and the Shakespeare they know is an American rock band! It is hard, as a parent, to move from the role of guardian and boss to seeing your teenager as a fellow human being deserving of respect. It is, after all, mutual respect that makes for a good relationship.

Accept that your teenager may be different to what you have wished for them, then prepare to let go of those hopes and expectations. In my long experience of counselling teenagers, they frequently comment that mum or dad want them to be something they are not. 'Dad just doesn't get it. I don't like maths and science. He can't believe that I'm not into all of that stuff. He keeps telling me over and over that I'd like it if I tried. I have tried it . . . and I don't like it! I like literature and history and he can't see the point of that stuff. It's hopeless!'

It's natural for parents to hope their children will appreciate the things they love. Sharing similar interests and beliefs makes it so much easier for us to 'connect' with others. So discovering that your teenager has very different interests and plans to yours is sometimes difficult to accept. It's hard to kiss that 'chip off the old block' mentality goodbye. But ultimately, if you respect your teenager's chosen ways to be an individual, rather than your ideal of them, they'll be a much happier person, and a more willing and successful student.

Maureen, mother of Kate, 16

My father put me on a horse when I was twelve. I promptly fell off and never got back on again. When my only child Kate came along quite late in my life, the last thing I expected was that she'd be mad about horses. We holidayed on a farm ten years ago. The girls there were horse riders and they put Kate on a pony. From then on, her interest in horses developed. It's all she thinks about and she has dozens of awards and trophies. You should see her room!

Kate and I are very different. It's been difficult to come to terms with this because we are light years away from each other interest-wise and even personality-wise. Kate is gregarious which I never was. As a child I adored reading and still love nothing more than curling up on the couch with a book. I teach senior literature and English. Kate doesn't read. My husband and I are both quiet. Kate's noisy. In fact, she's loud. Boisterous. When I'm feeling charitable I'd say she's 'feisty'; when I'm not feeling generous, I'd say she's 'aggressive'. At certain points we've had screaming rows. Sometimes we still do.

My husband gets involved in the horse riding a lot more than I do. He's out there with the saddles and blankets. I'm just not at home cleaning out a paddock. Kate used to wish I was more interested but I'm not a horsy person. Horses all look the same to me. Some of her friends' mothers are horsy women themselves and they've been fortunate that their daughters have followed on. Sometimes they even sleep in the horse floats! I can't do that. But I do what I can. Almost every day I'm driving her from one event or riding session to another and spend hours waiting in the car—with my corrections and a book, of course. I can't afford to retire because the horses cost so much! I'm working to support a horse.

Kate's never really liked school. She's not interested. She'll finish the final year at school but she's not travelling well. I've finally reached the stage where I can accept that she might not get a great score at the end of this year. As long as she's happy . . . And she is happy. She has a nice group of friends. She's not into drugs, drinking and parties. Horse riding is all she lives and breathes for. We're lucky she has something she's very good at.

She wasn't the child we expected. Even as a little girl she was quite different from my husband and I. But we've accepted each other. She's been a gift in my life and I love seeing her happy when she's riding.

Parent power:

- ◉ can lift or crush teenagers;
- ◉ shapes and moulds their perception of themselves;
- ◉ can help them develop high self-esteem;
- ◉ can be the defining factor in their ability to accept themselves;
- ◉ is an invisible force that can sustain and protect them;
- ◉ can help them do better at school;
- ◉ can help them develop a positive attitude to school and to life;
- ◉ can make them feel safe;
- ◉ can set them free to develop into secure and confident young adults.

In essence

For most people, parental expectations and acceptance are and will remain a significant driving force in all that they set out to accomplish in life. We all crave that our parents will look at us and show they are proud of us.

It is in listening to you and watching you handle the ups and downs of life that your teenager will form their own identity and ability to forge their way, both at school and in the world beyond. May the power be with you.

Setting an example is not the main means of influencing another; it is the only means.

—Albert Einstein

2

Using your influence wisely

Children have more need of models than of critics.

—Joseph Joubert

We have seen the enormous influence parent power can have on every aspect of your teenager's life. This chapter highlights five key ways in which parents can help teenagers to gain more out of school and life in general.

Equipping teenagers to get the most out of school

- Helping teenagers develop high self-esteem empowers them.
- Ensuring teenagers have a sensible perspective on education and intelligence gives them greater confidence.
- Nurturing teenagers' unique strengths and qualities enhances their enjoyment of school and life in general.
- Helping teenagers improve their skills strengthens their ability to tackle life's challenges.
- Helping teenagers nurture their passion reinforces their understanding of how motivation and commitment can bring achievement and satisfaction.
- Teenagers who are simply given everything never experience the thrill of discovering their own capabilities.

Promoting teenagers' self-esteem

Self-esteem is essentially how we feel about being ourselves. It's our ability to be comfortable in our skin. People with high self-esteem have a positive self-image and can accept their strengths and shortcomings.

How high or low your teenager's self-esteem is will greatly determine their ability to achieve success, socialise with others, form meaningful relationships and live a happy and productive life. Low self-esteem leaves teenagers vulnerable to peer pressure, stress, depression, high risk-taking and even suicide. Good self-esteem allows them to accept themselves and live life to the full. One of the best ways for teenagers to feel good about themselves is to know they are good at something. All teenagers have unique qualities and attributes worth cherishing. Sometimes parents need to help them discover, acknowledge and be proud of these qualities.

How is school affected?

High self-esteem gives teenagers the confidence to put in their best effort at school and often separates those who do well and those who don't. Students with high self-esteem don't crumble when they encounter problems, like being left out or having an attack of the zits right before the school social. For teenagers, perception becomes reality. Teenagers with little self-esteem don't believe in their capability and consequently don't put in much effort or give up altogether. Their negative belief becomes reality when they don't do well at school. Students with high self-esteem generally approach aspects of school—like homework, exams and sport—with a more positive outlook. Thinking success often leads to success. Why? Because high self-esteem leads to self-belief—that magical power that you can do anything, or at least give it a damn good shot!

I've often observed that teenagers who are bullied are those with low self-esteem. Those who believe in themselves and their abilities are more protected from the devastating effects of bullying. They're less vulnerable to peer pressure and voice their opinions confidently rather than being passive or aggressive. They generally get along better with people—peers and teachers—and this makes life

If you think you can or you think you can't, you're right.

—Henry Ford

more enjoyable and conducive to being able to relax, study and get the most out of school.

What can you do to enhance your teenager's self-esteem?

Accept them

Accepting your teenager unconditionally is the foundation upon which they can build self-esteem and accept themselves. Young people fearing rejection have a huge disadvantage at school. Sometimes teenagers have the *perception* that parents will be disappointed in them for various reasons—like not doing as well as an older sibling or failing to make the cricket team. Many parents I have counselled have been shocked to discover how worried their teenagers were about letting them down.

Teenagers afraid of disappointing parents or others often become insecure and stressed and lose confidence. Some become too shy to interact and participate fully in and out of class. Your unconditional acceptance will allow your teenager to pursue their interests, whether they be football or physics. Parental willingness to accept teenagers *as they are* also allows them to accept themselves and develop a positive identity.

Praise them

Don't economise when it comes to giving compliments. Show your appreciation of your teenager's talents and qualities. Don't focus solely on school results, though. If they feel good about any aspect of themselves, this generally results in a more positive attitude to school. It's easy to think teenagers know how much we value and appreciate them, but they often need to hear the words. 'We are so proud of Jason's results.' I've seen the effect these words can have on teenagers countless times—an instant pick-me-up.

Enhancing a teenager's self-esteem and positive attitude can come from the most unlikely source. Even winning a skateboard competition out of school provides a great opportunity to congratulate a teenager and make them feel good about themselves. An event like this can be a turning point for an insecure young person.

Empower them

Finding ways to help a shy teenager feel good about themselves can begin a transformation in them. If you think about it, often it's the little things that mean the most to us—those 'first times' we all remember so well. Don't wait until your teenager begs permission to try something new. Show you believe they are reliable and responsible by giving them opportunities to demonstrate it. By giving them a new level of responsibility *before* they ask for it, you're allowing them to feel appreciated and trusted. They'll love it!

Show that you value their opinions by listening to them and involving them in family decisions. Respect their opinions even if they're different from yours. It's a sign that you see them as young adults rather than as children.

Assume the worst and teenagers instantly know it, and often respond by letting you down for the hell of it. 'They don't trust me and I don't care.' Show your teenager you believe in them and they'll generally do better than measure up to your expectations: they'll surpass them and their self-esteem will skyrocket.

Give them permission to 'fail'

If you want your teenager to have high self-esteem, they need to accept that no one is good at everything. Teach them that what's important is having a positive attitude and giving life a go. Personal examples work well. Talk about goals you or family members and friends aspired to and perhaps never quite reached—but explain that what you discovered along the way made all the hard work worthwhile. Students who know they won't be sleeping in the garage if they 'bomb out' or are not the best at everything they attempt have greater confidence to accept new challenges at school and throughout life.

Teenagers with positive self-esteem:

- ⊚ are happier and generally more positive about school;
- ⊚ are prepared to try at school because they aren't afraid of 'failing';
- ⊚ are more realistic about their strengths and limitations;
- ⊚ generally get along with peers and teachers because they are happier and more confident;
- ⊚ are more protected from bullying;
- ⊚ form new relationships with others more easily;

- are more protected from negative peer pressure;
- cope better with setbacks of any kind—they don't resort to self-blame;
- have greater confidence when facing demands of homework and assignments;
- approach exams with greater confidence.

Teenagers with low self-esteem:

- don't have a positive self-image—'I'm no good at anything.'
- put themselves down—'I got an A but it was just luck.'
- stand back and are reluctant to try new things—'I could never do that.'
- see situations negatively—'I know I'm not going to do well on the exam.'
- are often shy and find it difficult to make friends—'She wouldn't like me anyway.'
- give up easily—'What's the point of trying? I won't be able to pass.'
- are sometimes loud and aggressive—even to the point of being bullies—as this is a way to hide their own insecurities and unhappiness—'This is a waste of time.'

Gaining insights into intelligence

Thankfully, the notion of intelligence has expanded beyond a simplistic focus on IQ and test scores alone. Concepts such as MI (multiple intelligences) and EQ (emotional intelligence) give a more comprehensive view of intelligence. EQ in particular has gained enormous credibility in the workplace. It's also often taken into consideration in selecting students for tertiary courses and for employment. Students should be made to be aware of this as it highlights the fact that scores alone are not the only important consideration. But before you can reassure your teenager, you need to be familiar with these ideas.

IQ

Most people have heard of IQ tests, but few realise that these focus mainly on verbal and mathematical skills.[1] It hardly seems right to judge a person's intelligence by such limited measures. That's what American neuropsychologist Howard Gardner thought too.

MI: Multiple intelligences

Gardner introduced the theory of multiple intelligences, proposing that there are at least *nine* different intelligences.[2] All are valuable for well-being and success.

1. linguistic intelligence;
2. logical-mathematical intelligence;
3. musical intelligence;
4. bodily-kinesthetic intelligence;
5. spatial or visual intelligence;
6. interpersonal intelligence;
7. intrapersonal intelligence;
8. naturalist intelligence;
9. existential intelligence.

Your teenager may be especially talented in one of these areas, or even several, and should feel proud of their achievements regardless of the particular area in which they excel. I've heard students say they are only good at art or sport as though this is something to be ashamed of. Students who are creative or great athletes deserve as much recognition as those who are good at mathematics.

But the two most under-rated areas in the minds of most students are the areas of interpersonal and intrapersonal intelligence. And, ironically, these are the two areas that are becoming more recognised by employers today.

Interpersonal intelligence involves the ability to understand others and what motivates them—the ability to empathise and get along with others.

Intrapersonal intelligence involves the ability to manage emotions, to understand yourself and to be able to identify and accept both your strengths and limitations.

EQ: Emotional intelligence

Daniel Goleman further developed Gardner's thinking on interpersonal and intrapersonal intelligence in his book, *Emotional Intelligence*.[3] Emotional intelligence is being aware of your feelings and the feelings of others. It's about motivating yourself and others, even when things go wrong. It's also about having empathy for others.

How is school affected?

Emotional intelligence is increasingly seen as the hallmark of successful leaders and managers. It is also fundamental in successfully managing relationships. This important knowledge can enhance students' self-esteem and encourage them to put in a greater effort at school. Students who don't excel in academic tests suddenly understand that there are other equally important attributes. Students who do excel in tests learn that they must also acquire other equally important skills. Suddenly the attention isn't on scores alone.

What can you do to help your teenager?

For various reasons, some people obtain high marks in exams while others don't. If you can convince your teenager that scores alone can't make or break their life, you'll do wonders for their self-esteem.

Getting the whole 'results thing' into perspective is a large task. 'What did you get?' is probably the question students ask each other most frequently. It's important to counter this results-focused approach. Telling teenagers about the many people who have been successful in life despite not doing well at school is very reassuring. I've often told students that Einstein failed to gain entry to an engineering course he had his heart set on; that Steven Spielberg was rejected by most of the prestigious film schools; that Australia's richest man, Kerry Packer, had problems at school and once described himself as 'academically stupid'; and that John Lennon's teachers described him as lazy.[4] Yet they all achieved in the world beyond school.

If your teenager comes home feeling disappointed with their results, reaffirm them. Show that what you value most is effort and attitude. Give the important message that hard work and determination are often the keys to success. Encouraging teenagers to focus on other intelligences in which they are more gifted is also a good way to encourage them. Students who believe they are failures often stop trying, and the self-fulfilling prophecy tightens its ugly grip.

You can be instrumental in helping your teenager to develop higher levels of MI and EQ. Focusing on interpersonal and intrapersonal intelligence will also help them to understand themselves more and relate better to others. Ironically, with the increased level of confidence this will bring, students of all abilities often obtain better results in tests.

It is not the IQ *but the* I WILL *that is most important in education.*
—Unknown

Part III of this book discusses qualities, attitudes and personal skills integral to interpersonal, intrapersonal and emotional intelligence, and highlights ways in which you can help your teenager to develop their abilities in these crucial areas.

Nurturing the positives

Everyone has abilities, strengths and gifts: it's simply a matter of discovering what these are and creating opportunities to develop them. I've seen students organise a function for 500 people, including booking the venue, ticketing, seating arrangements and catering. Others have the extraordinary gift of being calm in the face of emergencies and being able to lift the spirits of friends before stressful exam periods with their sense of humour and positive outlook. Other students excel in quiet but equally extraordinary ways. I suggested that one student undertake some voluntary work to develop his confidence. He applied to work for a few weekends at an aged-care hostel. Three years later he told me these were some of the 'best times' he had ever spent. This teenager's self-esteem had soared due to his experiences. These are all positives that uplift teens and make them feel good about themselves.

How is school affected?

Recognising, encouraging and praising teenagers' gifts and attributes is a great way to motivate them to work harder at school. Once young people experience success in *any* area, it often enhances their confidence and encourages them to put more effort into other areas of their life, both in and out of school.

What can you do to nurture your teenager's strengths?

Sometimes teenagers need help to appreciate their gifts. I've heard students say that they're no good at anything only to discover they're a trainee manager in their part-time job or develop websites for friends. Surprisingly, teenagers often don't recognise these as achievements. Point them out and celebrate them. Look beyond academic results. Nurture the areas in which your teenager displays an interest. Congratulate them if they've been selected for a sporting team or finally land a part-time job. The job may be stacking shelves, but for a young person it's a significant achievement. Show you're aware that part-time jobs are difficult to get and that you are impressed. Genuine praise and acknowledgment increase self-esteem and give teenagers courage to take up other challenges. Provide opportunities for them to develop gifts. Keep in mind that what's important to your teenager might not be what you regard as a high priority. Be involved in *their* interests.

Working on areas of need, vulnerabilities and limitations

Undoubtedly there are some areas in which your teenager could improve—perhaps study skills or interpersonal skills, or the ability to compromise or handle stress. No one is perfect. Instead of seeing these areas as weaknesses, teach your teenager to see them as *challenges*. One of the greatest gifts parents can give children is a positive attitude to adversity. Give them the support to work on areas of need. Inspire them to keep trying and not give up easily. The knowledge that you are on their side regardless of school results or successes in other areas of their life may inspire them to aim higher—to 'give it a go'.

What can you do to help your teenager address areas of need?

Find opportunities to help them

Many teenagers are highly self-critical and fear rejection. This prevents them from facing challenges head-on. Parents can engineer opportunities to allow teenagers to face challenging situations in a supportive environment. You are their safety net, encouraging them to fly through the air, to take that risk precisely because they know you're there to catch them should they fall.

If your teenager is shy, for example, help them to gain greater self-confidence by finding opportunities to enhance their interpersonal skills. Encourage them to take up short courses that complement existing interests. If they are creative, perhaps look for life-drawing or flower-arranging courses. In a non-competitive environment, the fear of failure is lessened and they're likely to gain a sense of achievement from the course itself. More importantly, they'll experience valuable inter-action with other people. *It's all about getting runs on the board.* It's from these small wins that bigger successes will follow. Soon they'll be less shy and more willing to give things a go of their own accord.

Approach with sensitivity

Don't put a spotlight on the area you believe your teenager needs to improve. For example, it's risky to tell them they need to be less shy. They're already painfully aware of this. A more diplomatic approach is better. Don't say, 'Paul, I think you should join in the school drama production this year. It would help you gain more confidence.' Something less direct has a much greater chance of success, like, 'Paul, when you were in primary school, you were so good at acting. Why don't you think of joining in the school drama production this year? It looks like a lot of fun.'

Be patient

Quick fixes are rare when it comes to improving your teenager's skills, atti-tudes or qualities; sometimes it takes years to acquire skills. Think back to when you were their age. (We all have things we'd prefer to forget!) It's impor-tant to acknowledge that your teenager is trying. Remind them of how they were unable to do this or that a year or two ago but can do it well now. Teenagers tend to forget how far they have come, just as the adults around them sometimes do. While it may resemble two steps forward and three steps back, encourage their efforts and allow them time to develop particular skills.

Helping them discover their passion

A passion is very different from an interest or hobby. It's that special something people know they're good at and love doing—something they can lose themselves in, like surfing, playing in a band, skateboarding, riding their horse (as it was for Kate in the last chapter) or spending the weekend buried in a book. Helping them to discover this decreases the chances they'll experiment in foolhardy ways to get a kick out of life. If their interest does move into dangerous areas—like violent computer games, gangs or computer hacking, discuss your concerns with them. Because teenagers sometimes won't listen to parents, know where to find support and who might be able to get through to them. Suggestions are outlined in Chapter 8.

How is school affected?

Whether teenagers enjoy academic life or not, having a passion is a fantastic self-esteem boost and gives them something to look forward to. If you've ever observed teenagers 'in the zone'—totally absorbed in an activity—you'll know what I mean. It's wonderful to see: shy students emerge from their shell; unmotivated students spark up. They've found something they can call their own and this ownership gives them a greater sense of self, of pride. Often the happiest students have special interests *outside* school.

Parents often worry that interests take valuable time away from study. On the contrary, students are increasingly at risk of burnout unless they have an outlet or hobby which allows them to switch off from school and relax. If you show genuine interest in their newfound passion, teenagers are more inclined to listen when you encourage them to also devote time to their studies. They're happier about themselves and often see school and other areas of life in a more positive light.

Acknowledge the effort your teenager is putting into their new interest and the fact that they have achieved something on their own. And, ultimately, this is precisely what teenagers crave—to be seen as individuals. Most teenage rebellion is about wanting to break away from adults and prove their individuality. If your teenager discovers something they're passionate about, often they won't have the need or the time to rebel. They'll be having too much fun!

What can parents do to help teenagers find their passion?

Sometimes teenagers discover it on their own—often at the least expected time and place. If not, here are some suggestions to consider:

- Pinpoint an existing interest or special talent and find ways to help them explore it. If they enjoy sport, try introducing them to a new sport; if they enjoy art, expose them to a new art form.
- If you see a new spark of interest, help foster it. Your teenager may meet up with someone who inspires them, or develop an interest after visiting an exhibition of, say, model cars, or watching a documentary on TV. Locate books, articles and ways they can become involved in this interest.
- Relatively inexpensive short courses exist in most interest areas. Investigate holiday programs and courses offered in your area.
- Involvement in social groups helps teenagers to make friends and discover new interests. Local councils are great sources of information about youth groups and clubs, sports associations, and so on.
- Be creative. Encourage your teenager to try new things. A strategy I've seen parents use successfully is giving birthday and Christmas presents which introduce new interests—a voucher for white-water rafting, cross-country skiing or a hospitality course. But don't sign your teenager up for abseiling if they're afraid of heights! The aim is to push the boundaries, not push them over the edge. And if you get it wrong and they totally 'freak out', why not use that abseiling voucher yourself! Come on . . . be adventurous!
- Keep your eyes open and encourage your teenager to try a variety of activities and experiences. When their eyes light up, you'll know they have found an absorbing passion.

Vital support for parents

We've suggested some ways you can help your teenager to perform better at school and become a happier and more confident person. Now it's time to look at the other side of the coin—you!

Take 'time out'

As your teenager needs 'time out' from schoolwork, you also need time for yourself. But it generally won't happen unless it's planned. Consciously make time for yourself, even if it's only a few hours a week. Whether you spend this time jogging, walking the dog or reading a good book, what's important is allowing time to unwind and regain valuable energy. You never know when you'll need to draw on this energy—your teenager may waltz through the door with multiple piercings or draped around a creature you barely recognise as human. Looking after yourself isn't a luxury; it's essential if you are to be emotionally prepared to care for your teenager.

Ditch the guilt

I'm continually amazed how often parents blame themselves if their teenager misbehaves at school or their results are lower than expected. Many parents feel particularly guilty about family situations around marriage break-ups, single-parent families, gay-couple parenting or financial difficulties and personal illness. Despite all I've said about your influence on your children, don't feel guilty about unavoidable circumstances. Teenagers today probably understand more about family dynamics than previous generations—they watch TV, surf the net and talk to friends. They're aware of various family compositions and interpersonal situations. So don't worry. It's all part of life—*real life*. Nobody lives the picture-perfect, Brady Bunch family life.

At the same time, if they have anxieties about such things, reassure them. We should never under-estimate how therapeutic talking is. A student recently saw me to inquire about special consideration for her exams due to her father's cancer treatment. She told me how much she wished her parents would talk to her more about her father's illness. 'They pretend it's okay but I can tell it's not true.' This student was so worried about what she was *not* being told that she was unable to sleep well or focus on her studies. When excluded from what is happening, teenagers generally imagine situations to be worse than they are.

It's not the type of family that matters, or even the circumstances. What counts most is your unconditional love, respect and trust. If you give your children this, they already have the greatest gift of all.

You're not alone

Chatting with other parents can be reassuring. You'll generally find they have similar concerns. Sharing the good and even the stressful times makes parenting less daunting. It shouldn't be a lonely business. 'Am I the only parent who worries like this?' a mother asked me. 'I worry that

I'm expecting too much or not doing enough to help. These are such important years and I don't know what to do.' Even her brief chat with me, the student counsellor, gave her a feeling of relief. It's important to have someone you can share concerns with. Joining a school committee is a great way to meet other parents regularly. If time prevents this, are there work colleagues who have teenagers or a friend or relative to confide in? Problems always appear more solvable when you share them.

FAQ: I continually feel guilty for not being able to spend more time with my teenage daughter, but this is impossible because of my personal situation. How can I make up for this?

A: Don't feel guilty if work prevents you from spending as much time as you would like with your teenager. There is something to the cliché of 'quality time'. Quality *is* more important than quantity. Spend time when you can and try to make it doing something your daughter enjoys. Talking to her honestly about your feelings may help both of you. Don't be surprised if she already understands and is not in any way feeling neglected. The very act of parents sharing feelings and concerns with teenagers can strengthen their relationship and pave the way for the teenager to, in turn, trust parents with their concerns. Part of growing up is accepting that life won't always be perfect and we need to make the most of the time and opportunities we have.

Diana and Carla, parents of Monica, 14

My partner and I decided to bite the bullet. We'd wanted to talk to our daughter for ages about whether our relationship was affecting her now that she was older. We've been raising Monica together since she was five. At primary school things were fine and Monica's friends would often come over after school or on weekends. Their parents would pick them up and meet Carla and me. I guess they knew we were a couple but we never actually talked about it. The topic never came up. We have always worried that things might be difficult during the teenage years and we were especially worried Monica might start to blame us for not having a 'normal' family.

Well, we took Monica to netball one Saturday as usual and after the game we all went to McDonald's for lunch. It's our family tradition. Right in the middle of our lunch, my partner brought up the subject. Thank God because I was thinking of chickening out and it had taken us so long to get up the courage to have that talk. Carla explained to Monica that we were worried she might be getting some flak from her friends about us. Carla went on to say that we would do everything we could to help and that we wanted her to know how important she was to us. We couldn't have been more surprised with her answer. 'You don't have to worry about me. You guys are great. I've only told my best friends at school and they're jealous because I'll have more clothes and makeup to borrow!' When I started to add that we loved her, she cut me off. 'I know mum. Chill out! I'm hungry. Can we get more fries?' And that was that.

Sophie Christou, parent

After my husband and I separated, my children and I had to start our lives from scratch. We had nothing. My daughter was 14 and my son 6. I sat down and explained to them that we wouldn't have the money to do most things they'd been used to doing. Do you know what they said? 'Mum, we just want you.' Since then I've run a restaurant to support us. Many times we only had the leftovers from the restaurant and the kids always worked for no pay. I remember one day driving in the car and my son asking me if I could get him a new pair of shoes some time. He was in high school then. It had taken him three months to tell me that his shoes were full of holes. He apologised for asking! He kept saying he could wait till I had the money. I cried when I saw the holes. We did it tough.

Today my daughter is finishing a Masters in psychology and Harry's worked in a few different areas and completed various courses. At 22 he's just announced he's going to uni to study astronomy. I'm so happy he's finally found what he wants to do. We're a very close family. They're the best kids. Material things aren't important to either of them. Love and care—they're the most important things for kids.

In essence

Parents have the ability to provide opportunities and support that can enhance a teenager's self-esteem and ability to be happy, and to make the most of their time at school. By showing your teenager that you believe school is not just about results, you teach them values that will help them throughout life.

> *If you want your children to improve, let them overhear the nice things you say about them to others.*
>
> —Haim Ginott

Part II
SECRET YOUTH BUSINESS
insights into the
teen world

3

Understand your teenager—mind, body and spirit

Trouble is, kids feel they have to shock their elders and each generation grows up into something harder to shock.

—Ben Lindsey

For many parents, the teenage years are a mystery. Why has my articulate John become a grunting stranger? Why does my Annie go around pretending she doesn't know me? Why do my kids act like I'm the most boring parent on earth? The mood swings, the silent treatment, the personality change by the second . . . we could go on. Yet many of us can remember a few of our own teenage antics and look back wondering, 'What the hell got into me?' In fact, there are explanations for this mysterious behaviour: they are the four challenges of adolescence.

The four challenges of adolescence

All teenagers must successfully negotiate these four challenges to emerge as adults. By understanding the challenges ahead of them, you'll know when to offer a supportive hand and when to give them space to take their own steps and ultimately find their place in the world.

As teenagers move through these crucial years, they look searchingly into the mirror of life, questioning themselves and the world around them.

Challenge 1: To form a positive sense of self, a positive identity

Teenagers try out different personalities and experiment to work out *who* they are. Teenagers who successfully complete this task mix more confidently and form more positive relationships. It allows them to be optimistic about life, to be more at peace and more resilient.

'Mirror, mirror . . . who am I? Do I suck? Do I pass or fail the ugly test?'

. . . Chaos and confusion rule!

Challenge 2: To establish independence from adults

In forging their identity, teenagers test the waters and contest previously accepted rules and opinions. They want to be heard and to make their own decisions.

'Mirror, mirror . . . why do I have to? You can't make me!'

. . . Rebellion rules!

Challenge 3: To form relationships outside the family

To establish emotional independence, teenagers need to form their own relationships. This begins with intense friendships, and graduates to deeper relationships with boyfriends and girlfriends. Ideally they want the whole enchilada: the I'm-in-love-with-that-one-special-person package.

'Mirror, mirror . . . why don't they like me? Do they love me?'

. . . Heartache rules!

Challenge 4: To find a place where they feel at home in the world

Completing this challenge involves making plans for the future and eventually becoming fully independent. It involves finding a career direction, becoming financially independent, confronting universal questions and making life-defining choices. With such vital challenges to negotiate, no wonder teenagers are somewhat conversationally challenged!

'Mirror, mirror...who am I? Where do I belong? What do I want out of life?'
... Decisions rule!

The three stages of adolescence

Teenagers have a precious few years to meet the four challenges. Psychologists refer to these years as the three stages of adolescence, but you probably know them as Hell.

Many parents lament: 'If they don't tell me anything, how can I help?' But the reality is that most teenagers won't voluntarily tell their parents what's going on in their heads. I've counselled countless teenagers and many more parents. What I can offer you is an opportunity to see into the world of today's teenagers *through their eyes*. I can help you translate the grunts and silences.

As a teacher and counsellor, I've heard it all. Day after day, students pour out their hearts—their concerns and dreams, their hopes and fears. When I ask, 'Do your parents know you feel like this?' the most common answer is 'Are you crazy? No way!' Even seemingly happy, high-achieving students often conceal insecurities, fears and resentment their parents would be staggered to hear about.

So what is going on in the heads and hearts of today's teenagers? What are the things teenagers tell me that they would *never* tell their parents? What are the things parents do and say—with all the best intentions in the world—that worry or annoy teenagers and diminish their enjoyment of what we often refer to as the best years of their lives? As we look at the three stages of adolescence, we will cover all of this.

Early adolescence: 8/10—14 years

Children officially join the Early Adolescent Club when they hit puberty and their hormones start wreaking havoc. Girls generally join earlier than boys, some as early as eight. Teenagers seem to grow centimetres overnight, bulge in previously flat areas and sprout pimples, hair and muscles before your very eyes.

The hallmark of early adolescence is physical change, and teenagers during this period are almost constantly preoccupied with what is happening to their bodies.

Leaving behind the familiarity and security of childhood isn't easy. They're entering foreign terrain trapped in a foreign body and they want to belong, to fit in. They knew the rules and the ropes of childhood, but this new Teen City contains huge question marks, new and daunting expectations. To make matters even more 'interesting', all these physical changes typically happen during one of the most difficult transitions your child has faced up to this point—the move from primary into high school. Physical and emotional change overload! It's no wonder your precious baby seems to have turned into a monster from Mars overnight. In essence, early adolescents suddenly find themselves unsure of where they belong and whether they're even normal.

What can parents expect?

- Early adolescents often feel confused and sometimes fearful about how they are changing physically.
- Typically, they start to break away from parents and to replace them with friends as their reference points. They want to be the same as their friends, and worry about being excluded or left out. At all costs, they want to belong.
- They're anxious to grow up without knowing what this means. They want to look older, dress older and act older.
- They're often moody, and begin challenging authority and previously accepted rules.
- This can be a scary time for parents. After all, overnight you've been replaced. The kid who used to adore you now worships the latest singing idol or the newest friend.

The million-dollar question for early adolescents is: 'Am I normal?' So what are typical early adolescent concerns?

A: 'Oh Tina you look sooooo good! How did you do it?'

B: 'The apple diet thingo. But I have to lose more. My legs are so huge.'

C: 'We're trying the lollipop diet... Gemma said it works if you stick to it for five days.'

A: 'What's a lollipop diet?'

B: 'Easy. Just lots of water and lollipops.'

Body Image

Body image is a hot issue for self-conscious teens. The influence of the media can be devastating for impressionable teenagers desperate to fit in. The deafening message is 'Thin is in!' and eating disorders are more common than you might believe (see Chapter 8 'What else is happening at school?' to learn how to identify signs of eating disorders). Conversations in the schoolyard frequently revolve around which diet is best, 'creative' ways to stop feeling hungry and how to tone up legs, thighs, bums and biceps.

Friendship

Who is talking to whom and who isn't, who is backstabbing whom, and who is 'in' the popular group or out is big news. Huge!

Claude, 13

The backstabbing got so bad that it made me sick and I stayed in bed for three days. Mum thought I had the flu but I was too upset to tell her the real reason. When I lost my best friend I felt like never going back to school. Parents don't think this is important, but it's important to us.

Mind benders for early adolescents

- ◎ 'Should my body look like this?'
- ◎ 'Does everyone else feel like this?'
- ◎ 'What's the right thing to say . . . do . . . act . . . wear?'
- ◎ 'Why do I feel like this?'

Mind benders: How do they affect studies?

Often teenagers are so 'hung up' about their appearance and trying to be part of the crowd that they lose focus on school. If your teen stands out in any way—is very tall or short, is markedly shy, has a lower or higher voice than most of their peers—be alert for signs of bullying and be ready to offer your support. Helping them to identify those special talents and interests we looked at in Chapter 2 will also provide a buffer during the tough times and boost self-esteem.

Deadly parental sins in this age group include:

- invading teenage privacy;
- drawing attention to physical changes;
- constant reminders about studies;
- not acknowledging they are growing up.

Wish list for early adolescents:

- the perfect body—(they're painfully self-conscious);
- to be accepted by friends, to fit in;
- greater independence and more privileges;
- to look sophisticated and in control.

What's changed since you were a teenager?

Teenagers today worry about relationships and sex earlier than previous generations did. Why? Check out images on billboards and in magazines. Teenagers are now bombarded with images that urge them to act more grown up. TV shows portray teenage romance and even teenage mother-hood—all prompting them to ponder about sex and relationships at increasingly younger ages.

They 'grow up' too quickly. They worry about the future and their chances of gaining high enough scores to enter university. It's not unusual for students who have barely found their feet at high school to begin asking whether the competition for tertiary places will be tougher for them compared to students today.

So what can you do to help your early adolescent? Here are some strategies to consider:

Be understanding

The best way to understand your teenager is to step into their shoes. Pick up a copy of the latest magazines teenagers adore, and be prepared for a shock or two if you've never done this. Yes, there is a huge emphasis on appearance. Yes, it's not always in the best taste. Remember those leg warmers or those flares you just had to have when you were 13? Your teenager's no different. Be understanding when they want to look exactly like their friends or the latest pop idol! This is simply part of the desperate need to fit in. It is enormously important to teenagers at this age, so avoid any criticisms of friends or the latest fads. Once again, it's all about allowing them to do what makes them feel good about themselves so that they are happier and are less distracted from studies and other important areas of life.

Within reason, accept their new dress sense (or lack thereof). Where you can, help them to be 'cool'. Let them have those shoes or that haircut if the budget allows. Teenagers can be cruel and appearance rules even in the school grounds. You don't want your child ostracised over a pair of sneakers.

Sometimes having 'unusual' interests, such as enjoying classical music or even being a high achiever, can result in a teenager being seen as a 'nerd' by their peers. I've known students who choose to forsake their talent or interest in order to fit in. It's wise to keep an eye out so you'll notice if your teenager is suddenly reluctant to engage in previously enjoyed interests or changes behaviour and seems unhappy about this.

Don't be afraid to openly discuss eating disorders, body image, fashion and other topics covered in teenage magazines. The best approach is to show interest without criticising. It helps to know a little about their world. Knowing the names of the latest items of clothing and fads will give you some credibility with your teen.

Be alert in case crazy diets are being followed and notice any changes in eating patterns. Encourage your teen to be fit and to eat healthy food rather than follow crash diets. Lead by example. Cook healthy, eat healthy and exercise regularly and you not only give teenagers a healthy outlook on life, but also lift your own spirits. If you believe your teenager may have or is developing an eating disorder, do not hesitate to contact an eating disorder clinic or support service in your area. There are experts who can provide you and your teenager with the right support and care.

And the ongoing friendship sagas? Treat them seriously. Be sympathetic and supportive. Teenagers who are torn apart over friendships generally aren't enthusiastic about their studies. Many students have cried in my office because the best friend isn't talking to them that day. Sometimes all they need is to *tell* someone. All parents need to ask is, 'Do you want to talk about it?' Teenagers may say no, but you've shown that you understand. And that's what counts.

Give them distance as they start working themselves out

Teenagers often say, 'Why do I have to respect their feelings when they don't respect mine!' If they want privacy in the bathroom, take it seriously. Knock first! If they don't want you to kiss them goodbye or even ruffle their hair in front of friends anymore, don't be offended. And if they want their room to be untouched, so be it. Cut them some slack. These are the things that can make a real difference to your relationship, and teenage energy can be redirected into studies.

Respect feelings and be sensitive about changes in appearance

Within reason, allow your teenager to be adventurous with things like clothes, makeup and hair. In the grand scheme of things these are not as important as your teenager's overall happiness and your relationship with them. I overheard an angry teenager say, 'My dad says I look ridiculous in makeup. The other day he threw all my makeup in the rubbish. It was mine.' Angry kids often break out by rebelling at school. Providing a safe, stable and loving environment at home is the best way to help them at school.

Don't constantly nag them about homework and study

One of the most common student laments is that parents are over-controlling about studies. 'Parents are always on your back about school. It makes us work less!' Even when I remind students that parents have their best interests at heart, they literally explode with, 'But it drives us crazy!' Most teenagers want space and more freedom, so sensitive comments that don't criticise but prompt them to take responsibility often work best. 'It's up to you to decide how well you want to do, because doing well will take hard work.' Monitor your teenager's reaction to gentle reminders and adjust your comments accordingly. (See Chapter 6 for an in-depth discussion of homework issues and strategies to support your teenager.)

Accept your teen unconditionally

At this stage, teenagers may question *everything*. They challenge previously accepted opinions, religious beliefs, family traditions and expectations. Ensure your teenager feels comfortable expressing opinions (regardless of how outrageous they are). Offering your opinion is important because teenagers need guidance from parents. But they also need unconditional acceptance as they enter this confusing period. Teenagers who feel unable to speak their mind at home only have their peers to shape their newly emerging thoughts. These peers may not be shaping your teenager in the most desirable way. Listen and discuss opinions with your teenager so that yours can be a formative influence as they test the waters with various philosophies of life. And students who can express their feelings and opinions at home generally have greater self-esteem and can focus more on their studies rather than warring with parents.

Middle adolescence: 15–17 years

Middle adolescence is a crucial time as it coincides with the senior years of school for most teenagers. At this stage, teenagers *worship* friends. Research shows that at no other time in our life are friends so important.[1] (See Chapter 8 for more discussion of the importance of friends.) Friends are the benchmark against which teenagers measure their success or failure as they try to work out who they are.

The hallmark of middle adolescence is the search for identity. This is the time for experimentation and rebellion! In searching for their identity, teenagers often appear to contradict themselves, sometimes changing their appearance, outlook and personality from one day to the next. More than ever, they need a 'significant other'—someone to rely on for advice and guidance. This significant person is often a relative—an older cousin, aunt, uncle or even a grandparent. It can sometimes be difficult for parents to push away feelings of inadequacy or envy when a child chooses to confide in another person, but this is simply part of the normal distancing from parents that comes with growing into an independent young adult. They will return.

It may comfort you to know that, throughout history, teenagers have 'entertained' parents with their seemingly irresistible urge to question and rebel against the status quo—and the parents have survived! As one rather famous but exasperated Greek citizen put it:

> *The young are permanently in a state resembling intoxication.*
>
> —Aristotle

What can parents expect?

Less sleep, fewer carefree days. *Lots of attitude!* In middle adolescence, teenagers try to work out who they are, what they feel and therefore what they want. They tend to challenge everything, to try everything and generally investigate every angle of the word 'rebel'! Typically, they persistently push boundaries as they seek to establish their own sense of control (identity). They want to break the rules.

The conformity that was the feature of early adolescence is replaced by individuality, which is often expressed through an array of ornaments, interesting clothing, language and makeup. Teenagers experiment with different appearances, behaviours and versions of themselves as they seek to find their comfort zone and establish who they are.

Understandably, some of the most common emotions these teenagers experience are curiosity, excitement and some anger. There is also sometimes ongoing confusion and fear at not living up to their own hopes and the hopes of their parents. Often the answering-back and the negativity are masks to hide feelings of insecurity. *These* are the times when teenagers most need sensitivity and support.

The million-dollar question for middle adolescents is: 'Who am I?' So what are typical middle adolescent concerns?

Parental nagging

Students at this stage constantly share horror stories about their parents. They compare how much their parents nag them about school and how little freedom they have. They want to be able to do things, go places and make decisions. 'Every time dad sees me I hear the same thing . . . when I was your age I was working already . . . why aren't you studying? . . . you don't know how lucky you are.'

Trust

Teenagers desperately want to be trusted and to feel that they have some control over decisions affecting them. Give them opportunities to make decisions, especially about school, so that they learn how to make good choices. Involve them in discussions. Avoid the 'when I was your age' stories. 'My parents won't let me do anything. I'm not a kid anymore. They don't understand that we want to do stuff. We want to make our own decisions. They even pick my subjects!' 'One minute they want you to do adult things but then they treat you like a kid.' 'How can we learn what to do if we can't try things ourselves? Parents should trust us more.'

Mind benders for middle adolescents

- ● 'Why won't people listen to me?'
- ● 'Why should I do what other people tell me?'
- ● 'What career am I interested in?'
- ● 'Will I get high enough scores to do a good course?'
- ● 'Do I have to be like my parents?'

Mind benders: How do they affect studies?

Teenagers who are all over the place emotionally often don't focus on school much. They're in 'no-man's land' as they question, experiment and try on different 'roles'. Who has time to study? They're busy negotiating the shifting terrain of friendships, trying to fit in and impress friends by challenging teachers and rules. I've seen teenagers do anything to stay part of the 'in crowd', including playing the 'I-couldn't-care-less-about-school' game. They are caught between the expectations of peers and parents/adults.

It is common for teenagers to question their sexuality at this stage.[2] 'Do I like girls, boys or both?' (See Chapter 8 for an in-depth discussion of relationships and sexuality.) I've seen numerous students whose results nosedive when they struggle to deal with issues surrounding sex and sexuality.

Deadly parental sins in this age group include:

- criticism of friends, choices or clothes;
- being over-controlling or over-protective;
- the most heinous sin—teenagers hate being told what to do!

Wish list for middle adolescents:

- friends! (even more important than in early adolescence);
- to be seen and heard!
- to be seen as rarely as possible in the company of their parents—they still need you to be there, though;
- greater independence and responsibility—they hate being treated like children.

What's changed since you were a teenager?

Today's increased media focus on high achievers, competition for places and rising unemployment has increased the fear of failure. Students increasingly talk about 'winners' and 'losers'.

Teenagers have greater access to legal and illegal drugs due to their wider availability. There's greater pressure to 'grow up', be experienced and 'sophisticated' at an early age. Marketing is deliberately aimed at teenagers in areas such as clothing, makeup and accessories—think of the huge range of teenage mobile phones around.

So what can you do to help your middle adolescent?

Be firm but fair

Allowing teenagers new freedoms doesn't mean a free-for-all at home. Teenagers need boundaries but make them reasonable and stick to them. Students unable to accept expectations or standards at home find it harder to accept rules and regulations at school and in the workplace.

Be willing to listen and negotiate

Remember, the home climate affects school temperatures. I've lost count of the number of students whose schoolwork grinds to a halt if they are grounded or tension escalates at home. 'My dad full on yells at me!' 'My mum lectures me!' If possible, approach conversations calmly and with a positive attitude, *regardless of what's happened*. You don't want your teenager to be spending more time offloading to friends about how 'unfair' you are than concentrating on their studies.

Loosen the parental reins

Acknowledge that they are growing up by giving them greater freedom and more responsibilities. Start with small independence-forming experiences and allow them to expand their wings. Allow them to come home later on special occasions, to travel independently to a sporting event with friends or attend that desperately important party. You're preparing them—and yourself—for the day when you can let go and they can take bigger steps on their own. You're showing them that you acknowledge they are growing up. Part of this process involves allowing them to make those little and large mistakes we all make. Teenagers who feel trusted and respected by parents generally have more confidence in all areas, especially with their studies.

Stay informed

Make it a daily event to ask how school is going but, to avoid hearing the same old grunt or 'fine' response, ask specific questions, like 'Is English interesting this year?' or 'What are you covering in history this term?' This is the time when decisions have to be made about subject choices and career directions. If you can maintain a close relationship with your teenager, you will be able to support them with these important choices.

If tensions escalate too much over any personal issues, teenagers often lose focus on their studies. The secret is to work on keeping the peace at home so that communication channels are open and you can offer encouragement and support. It's also a great idea to be alert and on the lookout for signs of unhappiness or stress. (See Chapter 9 for ways to address specific issues such as bullying, losing motivation, failing at school or wanting to leave school early.)

Get to know their friends (even the 'friends from hell')

You can learn a lot about teenagers from looking at their friends. Are they ambitious, generous, socially responsible, thoughtless or reckless? I know many teenagers who look an absolute fright but they're harmless. Look beyond the hair gel and the Goth gear. *Talk* to their friends, *listen* to them and *don't judge them*. Make them welcome in your home. By accepting your teenager's friends, you'll also see much more of them during this period.

But what if you believe your teenager's friends are a danger? Discuss this with your teenager. Despite the fact that teenagers often seem to ignore parents, they generally take in what you say—especially if you discuss issues without criticising them. Should you ban friends? Only as a last desperate measure; you risk driving your teenager into their company even more. Banishing friends may well alienate your teenager from you. Unfortunately, some teenagers have to experience things for themselves before they come to a decision that is remarkably similar to the one you wanted them to make anyway. But you can diplomatically lead your teenager to see friends in their true colours. Table 3.1 provides a few examples.

Table 3.1 The right moves

Risky stuff	Smart move
'I'm sick of hearing that ape of a friend of yours make fun of you. Jason's an idiot! You should have more sense than putting up with his stupid remarks.' (Guaranteed to annoy your teenager and also a personal criticism.)	'Jason's a funny guy. He makes everyone laugh. I wonder if he realises that he might offend some people, though . . . Can he take jokes about himself?'
'Susan is such a user. Why do you put up with her? I've never once heard her thank you. Why don't you get some decent friends?' (Sure to anger and it's another criticism of your teenager.)	'I think it's great that you help Susan so much with her work. I'm sure she appreciates what you do for her. She's so lucky to have a friend like you.'
'Why do you waste time with Frank and Jack? Those losers obviously aren't interested in their future at all. I thought you had more sense than that!' (Guaranteed to annoy and alienate.)	'Frank and Jack seem pretty relaxed about the exams. Have they decided what they want to do next year? What do they think about your plans?'

Late adolescence: 18 to when they become almost completely independent

In late adolescence, teenagers seriously grapple with their identity. The hallmark of late adolescence is decisions and more decisions. Teenagers are working out the universal life questions: what they believe; what the purpose of life is; what's important to them. No wonder they sometimes seem preoccupied! Some adults still haven't quite figured out these answers.

Late adolescence occurs when most teenagers face a huge transition in their life—moving into the world beyond high school. To do this successfully requires the ability to negotiate new settings, challenges and demands. Chapters 10 and 11 cover practical ways to prepare teenagers to leave school with greater confidence and optimism.

What can parents expect?

The good news is that this is when most teenagers again begin believing their parents aren't so bad after all, but instead can be valuable allies. Hallelujah! It's important to make time to be with teenagers at this stage and to discuss emerging ideas and choices with them.

The first few years after leaving high school are challenging for emotionally vulnerable teenagers. Some fly ahead while others flounder. It can be a scary and uncertain world for them, so be alert for signs that they are struggling.

Among the most common emotions late adolescents experience are excitement, anticipation, anxiety and fear about their future.

The million-dollar question for late adolescents is: 'What is my place in the world?' So what are typical late adolescent concerns?
- Leaving school and facing the uncertainties ahead.
- Possible unemployment.
- Making the right course/career/job choice.
- Somehow missing the boat in life.
- 'I've worked so hard at school and now I'm scared I'll mess everything up by making a bad decision.'

- 'All of my friends know what they want to do and that's scary because I'm the only one who doesn't.'
- 'Should I do further study/travel/work?'
- 'Will I make new friends or lose all my school friends?'

Mind benders for late adolescents

- 'What do I want out of life?'
- 'What do I feel passionate about?'
- 'What do I want to do with my life?'

Mind benders: How do they affect studies and work?

These are huge questions. If young people are over-worried about them, they will obviously be unable to have adequate headspace to concentrate on studies or that new job. Be there for them and make your unconditional support crystal clear. But you've got to mean it. Countless young people have told me that parents say they support their decisions, but they don't believe them. If your teenager sees disappointment in your face, your words become meaningless.

Deadly parental sins in this age group include:
- being over-protective;
- under-estimating the stress involved during the adjustment period after high school.

Wish list for late adolescents:

- greater independence and respect;
- a soul mate, meaningful relationship or friend they can count on;
- to find their niche (course, job);
- to feel their life has a purpose.

What's changed since you were a teenager?

With the escalating costs of higher education and housing, many young people live at home longer. While this is not intrinsically undesirable, it delays the time when they become more independent. Although many are able to be independent while living at home, they are not completely responsible for the myriad things that come with moving into a separate living arrangement. In a real sense, this does delay their 'growing up' and the satisfaction of making it on their own.

Careers are appearing, disappearing and being revolutionised before their eyes. Today's world is fast moving and unpredictable. All of this can worry teenagers. To add to this, globalisation, constantly changing technology and terrorism have made the world a generally less predictable and more risky place.

So what can you do to help your late adolescent?

Treat your teenager as an adult

In middle adolescence, teenagers test their wings. As they leave school, they need more than this. *Let your teenager fly!* Whatever you do, don't hold them back. It's important for teenagers to learn to stand on their own feet, to take responsibility and to make important choices. Be there as a supporter and a backstop, but allow your teenager to make the calls.

Accept their choices

Rather than saying 'It's the wrong choice' or 'I don't think you realise what you're doing', try to be a sounding board. Ask questions that make your teenager think, but not questions that are thinly veiled criticisms. Young people hate it when adults ram opinions down their throats. Often that's why they turn to their friends so much: friends generally listen without criticising. Respect their views and they may respect yours too.

Be supportive around transition times

Young people find it particularly hard to admit they are scared. Yet the move from high school to further studies or into the workforce can be daunting. Be vigilant and look for signs that your teenager may need to talk things through or simply to know that you realise these are big moments in their life.

Some parents feel that their worries are over when their teenagers are safely in tertiary studies or employment (see Chapter 12). While many are in this fortunate position, never assume all is well. Rising levels of youth depression and suicide are warning signs that all is not well with many late adolescents. Ex-students frequently tell me how much they miss the security and familiarity of high school. Many feel lost and unsure. Be around to talk about things and offer your reassurance and support, regardless of their results or life decisions.

Whether teenagers leave high school early to go into employment or another form of study such as vocational study, or complete high school before going into further study or employment, they face a potentially stressful time unless they are offered suitable support. A very encouraging recent report, *The Landscape of Support for Youth in Transition*, highlights that there are numerous high schools, agencies, vocational institutions and universities offering excellent support and programs to assist young people in periods of transition.[3] Parents can help teenagers enormously by being aware of the many avenues of support available.

While much that lies ahead for young people is unpredictable, some things—like parental support and acceptance—should be 100 per cent guaranteed. If teenagers come home with a disappointing result or face other setbacks, this is the time for parents to encourage them and help them move forward. If friends disappoint them, this is the time for parents to offer reassurance. In an uncertain world, support from home is the most stabilising influence a young adult can have.

In essence

Understanding what is going on in your teenager's head helps you support them through the challenges of adolescence. The best way to help your teenager through the stages of adolescence is to maintain and strengthen your relationship with them. Chapter 4 covers this important area in more detail.

The best way to make children good is to make them happy.

—Oscar Wilde

4

Helping your teenager thrive

The old believe everything; the middle-aged suspect everything; the young know everything.

—Oscar Wilde

It takes a great deal of time, energy and emotional investment to create a positive parent–child relationship. With hormones raging and personalities changing, sometimes it's hard to even recognise your child, let alone having a meaningful relationship with them!

Let's look at some tried and tested ways to maintain a positive relationship with your teenager and examine how these strategies impact on their schooling.

Some ways to strengthen relationships with teenagers include:

- communicating;
- avoiding duels;
- avoiding personal criticisms;
- ignoring as many of the negatives as humanly possible;
- forgiving the past;
- providing opportunities for teenagers to feel good about themselves;
- respecting teenagers' feelings, opinions and choices;
- respecting their privacy;
- being involved in their lives;
- treating them as adults.

Communicate

Open communication is the bedrock of positive relationships. It is the key to successful parenting. I've been in many discussions with parents and students where so much is left *unspoken* between them. Both parties assume silence can be correctly interpreted as though by mental telepathy. Instead, misunderstandings mount and frustration bubbles over. I've had to facilitate many times to help bring silent warring parties together. 'Robert, how about telling your mum how you feel about what's happened recently' or 'Karen, I think your dad would like to tell you why he's been so worried about you.'

Many headaches are solved when two parties put all their emotional cards on the table. Ask your teenager how they feel about issues, events or whatever is happening in their life. 'How are things going at school? How do you feel about X? What can we do to help out?'

Here are some strategies to consider:

See things from their perspective

This increases the chance that they'll try seeing things from your perspective.

> **Rather than**: 'Are you serious? There are only two weeks to go before your exams and you're going to waste valuable time.'
> **Try**: 'I can see how important this party is to you but there are only two weeks to go before your final exams. Are you sure you can afford the time to go? You're the only one who can judge what's best.'

Ditch sarcasm, nagging and threats

Diplomacy wins hands down. And humour is a wonderful way to defuse a tense situation.

> **Rather than**: 'If you ever come home this late again you're grounded for the rest of the year! I'm sick of your broken promises. I just can't rely on you!'

Try: 'I'm too frazzled to sit home worrying about you until the early hours of the morning. My nerves can't take the strain. I care about you and don't want anything to happen to you. All I want you to do is call if you're going to be home late.'

Rather than: 'Do you have any idea how selfish you are? I'm sick of your inconsiderate attitude. If you can't keep your end of the bargain and get home when you promise, you can forget going out at all!'

Try: 'It's cost me a fortune to look after you all these years and I want you to stay in one piece. You're way too valuable and gorgeous for me to risk having damaged.'

Of course, saying all of this with a smile is the icing on the cake. And the golden rule is: *never* embarrass teenagers by telling them off in front of their friends.

Things parents shouldn't say:

- ◎ 'I'm older and I understand these things better than you.'
- ◎ 'While you live under my roof, you'll do as I say or get out.' (Never threaten. I know one student who left home after a similar comment.)
- ◎ 'You're too young to understand.' (Implies their opinions are irrelevant.)
- ◎ 'I've made a decision and that's that', or 'You'll do as I say'. (Teenagers detest injustice. Avoid using tyrannical statements.)
- ◎ 'I know better than you.' (This will only annoy a teenager and hurt their pride.)
- ◎ 'I know what's best for you.' (How would you feel if someone said this to you? Guaranteed to annoy!)

How is school affected?

Teenagers learn by parental example. Open communication at home leads to open communication at school. Students who can confidently express themselves at home and listen to other opinions will form more positive relationships with peers and teachers. These teenagers have an edge both in and out of school (see Chapter 5).

Avoid duels

Resist being drawn into unpleasant verbal duels with your teenager, regardless of how angry or disappointed you are. Duels only end in shouting and slammed doors, with no resolutions or closure. If teenagers return three hours later than promised, 'forget' to tell you about parent–teacher night or are suspended yet again, don't pounce the second they come home. Find the right time to sit down and sort things out. It's a great way to show you still love them and helps to keep them on track (see Chapter 7).

How is school affected?

Angry shouting matches at home tend to spill over into school. In my experience, many students 'act out' at school—swearing, refusing to follow instructions, answering in an unacceptable tone of voice—because they're upset about ongoing and unresolved conflicts at home. Just as teenagers learn how to communicate openly from parents, they use verbal duels to resolve issues if it is the predominant method used at home. This antagonises teachers and peers and affects student happiness.

Avoid personal criticisms

Inevitably, teenagers make mistakes. When this happens, focus on the *behaviour* you'd like changed. Delivering a message *minus* personal attacks makes it less threatening and more acceptable to a sensitive teenager. 'I' statements are effective.

Rather than: 'John, are you stupid or something! This is the second time you've been given detention this term. Why do you insist on asking for trouble? What do you have to say for yourself?'

Try: 'John, I care about you and I'm worried that things don't seem to be going well at school. What can I do to help?'

Rather than: 'You are a lazy, inconsiderate lump. You're always leaving your mess for me to clean up!'
Try: 'I feel hurt when you leave your mess for me to clean up. Please ask me if you don't have time yourself.'

How is school affected?

Teens who can differentiate between the mistakes they make and their intrinsic capabilities learn from these mistakes and move on with their self-esteem intact. They understand that making mistakes does not indicate stupidity.

Avoiding personal criticisms becomes increasingly important as teenagers get older because choices or perceived 'mistakes' become weightier. I have found that, as the stakes rise in the senior years, students who are afraid of failing or disappointing their parents, sometimes hold back or stop trying altogether.

Ignore as many of the negatives as humanly possible

There may be a million and one things your teenager does that drive you to distraction. However, you'll never survive if you attempt to tackle all of them. Sometimes it's better to turn a blind eye to minor issues that are not earth shattering. You can adjust to having a daughter with unusual hair or a son who appears to be averse to conventional clothes or even wearing shoes. If teenagers are happy, does it really matter if they look more 'interesting' than you'd prefer? Save your energy for battles that are worth fighting.

This does *not* mean that you have no boundaries or expectations. While you may be flexible about trivialities such as dress, teenagers should respect family 'rules' and the rights and feelings of family members. Relationships must be built on mutual respect and teenagers need to learn this. Learning to accept rules that are non-negotiable can save teenagers from much angst at school, where certain rules must be obeyed.

> **Rather than**: 'You'll be home when I say or you can forget going at all.'
>
> **Try**: 'We expect you to be home before midnight and to contact us if you will be late so that we won't worry unnecessarily.'

How is school affected?

Teenagers often detest parental insistence that they clean under the bed, hang up the towels or put away their shoes. Conflict over minor issues can take their focus away from studies and more important concerns.

Forgive the past

Keeping a tally of major crimes and misdemeanours only causes resentment. Many teenagers already believe that adults hold grudges. *Telling* teenagers incidents are over reassures them and frees them to move on.

> **Rather than**: 'If you think I'm going to forget this you have another thing coming.'
>
> **Try**: 'This has been a learning experience for both of us but it's over now and I know I can trust you not to let it happen again.'

How is school affected?

Teenagers able to forgive, forget and move on after any conflict avoid much unnecessary angst. Being able to give and take, and of course saying sorry, are invaluable skills for all teenagers. Students who can get along with each other and with their teachers are generally happier at school. (See Chapter 8 for strategies to help teenagers manage conflict.)

Provide opportunities for teenagers to feel good about themselves

Making teenagers responsible for aspects of their life teaches them to handle responsibility and boosts self-esteem. I know teenagers who look after the neighbour's pets and garden while they're away on holiday; others look after younger siblings until their parents arrive home. Another student I teach is responsible for entering data for his mum's home business several hours a week. Teenagers love being able to prove themselves.

> **Rather than**: 'I hope you're doing a good job because I can't afford you to mess things up.'
> **Try**: 'I'm impressed with the way you have hopped in and accepted this new responsibility. Good on you.'

How is school affected?

Students who have tasted what it's like to feel trusted and responsible for something shine in leadership positions at school. They have the confidence to apply in the first place.

Respect teenagers' feelings, opinions and choices

Most teenagers are allergic to the 'mother/father/teacher knows best' message. They crave being heard and seen as individuals. Forcing your own views of the world on them usually backfires. Show interest in their opinions, even if you view things differently.

Try to see things through the eyes of your teenager. What may seem trivial to an adult can be an enormous setback to a young person. Don't trivialise something that upsets your teenager. A fight with a friend, a betrayal of trust, the loss of a relationship—these can be traumatic events for a teenager. And avoid throwaway statements like, 'Don't worry, there are plenty of fish in the sea'. When you're 14, it feels like the fish that got away is the only worthwhile fish.

Parental patience and understanding can help teenagers enormously. So resist the temptation to hit the roof if your teenager strides into the house sporting a newly pierced eyebrow. 'My God, what on earth have you done to yourself!' is only going to hurt feelings and cause resentment.

Karen, 15

I received a phone call from a father who was trying to decide whether or not to send his daughter to the school where I teach. She had received a partial scholarship to another school further away and a decision had to be made.

Parent: Hello, I'm Peter and this is Karen. Unfortunately my wife couldn't be here today as she has just started a new job.

Me: Nice to meet you (shakes hands with both).

Parent: As I explained on the phone, we have to decide which school to enrol Karen in. We're new to this area and would like to know more about this school before we make a decision. Karen's been doing very well at school. Maybe she is the best person to explain all of this and ask you what we need to know . . .

Jason, 15

Jason is a tall boy with straggly brown hair covering most of his eyes and face. From what I can see through the hair, he looks very annoyed at being dragged into my office by his mother. He sits slouched down in the chair staring at the floor or occasionally at the space immediately above my head.

Parent: (Comes forward and shakes my hand) Thanks for seeing me. I want to check that Jason has his facts right. He's been telling us that he doesn't need physics to be an architect and his father and I are concerned. In fact, we'd like him to continue with both physics and chemistry. Jason doesn't always tell us the whole story and he sometimes only hears what suits him. He tends to be lazy and drops anything as soon as it becomes difficult. We're still disappointed that he gave up playing the piano. (Jason rolls his eyes at this point.) Anyway, we want to check that he's not limiting his options by taking the easy way out. We don't think he understands how important it is to have the right subjects.

Me: Well, Jason and I had a long talk about courses and pre-requisites a few days ago.

Parent: I see. Of course, he never tells us anything . . .

How is school affected?

I've conducted hundreds of interviews with parents and students present together. Teenagers who feel respected by their parents generally have a confidence and energy others lack. They are more at ease in school and less inclined to tune out or play up. The stories of Karen and Jason are two examples of the many conversations that remain vivid in my memory. Imagine how you'd feel if you were the teenager in these scenes.

I can't remember what Karen said word for word. What I can remember is the relaxed and comfortable bond between father and daughter. Karen was actively involved in the decision-making and her parents were clearly happy to support *her* final choice. For a teenager of 15, Karen was a confident speaker. She was clearly accustomed to discussing concerns with her parents. What stood out was the mutual respect evident between father and daughter.

And Jason? Perhaps he was unspeakably obnoxious at home despite the concern of his parents. Perhaps he'd hooked up with a 'bad lot' of friends and was driving his parents to distraction. But whatever causes tension between teenagers and parents, when respect disappears, so does any hope of a positive relationship. However impossible teenagers may be at home, it's never wise to reveal their personal foibles to a teacher, a friend or anyone else for that matter—especially if the teenager in question is present. No one likes to be talked about as though they aren't there. For a self-conscious teenager, this is not only excruciatingly embarrassing, but is tantamount to betrayal.

Teenagers crave the respect and approval of their parents. Mutual respect between Jason and his parents had become a casualty in what appeared to be an ongoing war. In a situation like this, parents must take the initiative and call a 'ceasefire'. Even if teenagers regret something they've done or said, they rarely make the move to reconcile. Teenage pride is legendary. Parents generally have to be the bigger people—even when your teenager towers above them—and call for time out. It's so important to keep mending those bridges between yourself and your teenager. The Jasons of this world often feel so angry that they don't want to perform their best at school, while the Karens are streets ahead.

Respect their privacy

Teenagers jealously guard their privacy. It's a way of visibly signalling that they are no longer children and deserve adult privileges. Many parents have told me that this privacy phenomenon happens overnight. There's no adjustment time, no mercy shown to those who offend and no turning back the clock. Some teenagers even post a 'Keep Out' warning on their door. But sign or no sign, respecting teenagers' privacy is essential.

How is school affected?

One of the bitterest comments I hear from teenagers is that their privacy isn't respected at home. This wastes your teenager's emotional energy. It yields no brownie points for you (just more laundry). Indignation tends to affect a teenager's focus on studies.

Be involved in their lives

Having a good relationship with your teenager makes it less likely they will engage in negative behaviour such as becoming the class clown, swearing or becoming involved in other antisocial antics. Spend time with your teenager and offer to do things that are important to them, such as having the end-of-term party in your home. Unsolicited, unexpected offers are amazingly effective ways to show your interest and support.

How is school affected?

When parents watch their teenagers run in a race or act in a school play, this encourages them to take up other opportunities both in and out of school.

Treat them as adults

Ultimately, this is what teenagers crave. They go to extraordinary lengths to prove to the world that they've grown up. Giving teenagers greater freedom generally lessens their need to challenge adults and make those infamous statements: 'Why should I do what you say? What would you know!' or 'You can't make me'. Acknowledging that your teenager is becoming an adult and that you want to relate to them on a different level increases the chances they will respond in a more mature manner. The relationship you establish now with this newly emerging young adult forms the basis of your ongoing relationship with them.

Make it a relationship based on mutual respect and it could remain a lifelong bond.

It's important to accept that, as they get older and want more freedom, the nature of the relationship parents have with their children changes. Parents don't become obsolete; they simply take an important step into the background, allowing children the space to grow up. Parents remain the home base they'll return to many times over as they move through life.

How is school affected?

Students who are accustomed to relating positively to adults, such as parents, have an inner confidence and ability to relate positively to peers and teachers and to make more sensible choices.

When there's tension with parents

Countless students have told me that their parents don't know them as well as their friends do. Teenagers want parents to take more time to listen to them, to understand their feelings and opinions. And they say these things with real regret. Many teenagers could perform better at school if these concerns were addressed. In fact, many stop studying or rebel out of a sense of frustration. Following are some of the most common sentiments I hear students express over and over.

What's going on inside teenage heads?

Teenspeak: 'Mum listens to me but I know her mind is already made up. It's a waste of time even talking. Parents always say that one day we'll thank them for making us do what they say. Yeah right!'
Translation: 'I'm angry because I want to be listened to.'

There will be times when no compromise is possible and as a parent you must make the decision you believe is best for your child. But *always* take the time to first carefully listen to teenagers and respect their right to hold opinions that differ from yours. And teenagers can identify the precise second when adults have switched off. 'I understand', 'I can see why you might feel like this' and 'I'm sorry you have been hurt' are some responses that show adults are listening to a young person. Many teenagers will accept a decision that goes against their wishes if they have been given the opportunity to be heard and acknowledged.

Teenspeak: 'Why do parents always think things were more difficult for them than us? They have no idea.'
Translation: 'I worry about different things.'

Avoid comparing your experiences to those of your teenager, and stay informed about issues affecting teenagers today. Be sympathetic rather than judgmental. Think about the things that worry teenagers: unemployment, exams, getting a part-time job, finding a date for the school dance or the state of the environment. Every teenager is different. What causes yours to toss and turn at night?

Teenspeak: 'Parents always think they're right!'
Translation: 'I want my opinions to be treated with respect too!'

Discuss, compromise and sometimes even be prepared to say you have made a mistake or over-reacted (we all do). Teenagers love it when adults apologise to them. For most it's a novelty.

Teenspeak: 'We can't do anything! They treat us like kids' or 'Parents don't trust us!'
Translation: 'I'm not a child anymore.'

All parents have various 'rules' or expectations. Do a stocktake. Can any of the 'No ways' be renegotiated? What about compromises? Has your teenager grown up since the 'rule' was introduced? Was it made in the heat of the moment or after a disastrous teenage stuff-up? Sometimes re-drawing the line in the sand demonstrates a renewed faith in teenagers.

> **Teenspeak**: 'I know I'm a disappointment to my parents. It's never good enough. They don't say it but you can tell' or 'Dad and mum want a lot for me. It's scary. I just can't be as good as they want.'
> **Translation**: 'I'm stressed and worried about letting my parents down.'

I've even heard the highest-achieving students say this! It's crucial to *say* you are proud of results and achievements. Misunderstandings prevent some great kids from being happier at school. Don't let it happen in your home.

What's going on inside parents' heads?

Countless parents have also expressed concerns to me about their teenagers. Sometimes it's reassuring to know that you are not the only parent with concerns and that the issues you are facing are the typical parent bugbears. (Specific issues relating to school performance and frequently asked questions are addressed in detail in Chapters 7, 8 and 9.) Here are some common parental concerns:

> **Parent**: 'My teenager doesn't listen to me anymore. I'm never right while their friends can do no wrong.'
> **Translation**: 'I'm scared of losing my central place in their world.'

As children grow up, they're inevitably going to expand their social circle and be influenced by it. Remember that teenagers grapple with making sense of *who* they are and consequently challenge those around them. Don't take it to heart if your teenager appears to idolise everyone but you—it will pass! Eventually teenagers will 'return'—especially closer to the age when they need to learn how to drive!

> **Parent**: 'Teenagers seem to think the world revolves around them. They don't realise that parents have commitments and problems too.'
> **Translation**: 'I'm tired. What about me?'

Teenagers need to understand that parents are busy and have responsibilities. Part of growing up is *learning* to be considerate so don't be afraid to discuss an issue—calmly—with your teenager. Make time for yourself; being a supportive parent requires enormous emotional energy.

> **Parent**: 'I want to help but I'm unsure of what to do and say anymore. My teenager won't tell me anything.'
> **Translation**: 'Help!'

All teenagers are different, though girls generally start to become secretive while boys typically show bravado and challenge authority to prove their manliness. Some teenagers cope with occasional cathartic explosions to let off steam while others internalise everything. Which is your teenager inclined to do? All teenagers need someone they can offload to—a friend, a teacher or a grandparent. Some parents quietly ask one of these people to casually chat to their teenager. It also helps to find opportunities to share quality time with your teenager, even if it has to be over an occasional McDonald's meal.

Above all, be supportive regarding school. It takes up a huge part of a teenager's life and anything parents can do to make it as pleasant as possible will contribute to their overall happiness.

In essence

Most students I counsel who are angry, depressed or apathetic believe they have no choices and no voice in whatever is affecting them. Empower your teenager by giving them real choices as they start tackling the big questions in life. Maintaining a positive relationship with teenagers is the most secure safety net they can have.

In all things we learn only from those we love.
—Johann Wolfgang von Goethe

Part III

MORE THAN A PACKED LUNCH

giving your teenager the edge

5 ❁

The kitbag for success

If we all did the things we are capable of, we would astound ourselves.

—Thomas Edison

We introduced the skills, attitudes and attributes for success (SAAS) in Chapter 1—skills such as confidence, self-esteem, optimism, good communication, conflict management and leadership ability. With these in their kitbag, teenagers can fly through high school and life beyond it. In school, as in life, the happiest people are those who are confident and have a positive outlook on life. Indeed, research shows that teenagers who feel better about themselves are less likely to feel a need to prove themselves in negative ways.[1]

How can parents help teenagers fill their kitbag for success?

Unfortunately, this kitbag can't be purchased along with school textbooks. Most skills, attitudes and attributes require time to develop, but it's never too late or too early to guide your teen. Parents are the most important teachers of all. What you teach your teenager can never be gained solely from school. Teenagers acquire the ability to empathise, as well as resilience and the ability to set and achieve goals, when they see parents demonstrating these qualities. If parents continually bemoan the unfairness of the world, how can their teens learn optimism? Like a sponge, teenagers absorb all the positives and negatives parents impart.

Activities to help teenagers thrive

One of the best ways to supplement their kitbag and for them to acquire and improve these skills is through exposure to new challenges and opportunities. Be on the lookout for new activities that may appeal to your teenager. Lead by example and try out new activities with them.

In unfamiliar situations, teens have to stretch and test their kitbag of skills. Whatever the situation—a new part-time job, a new basketball team or a new musical production—they'll confront similar challenges. They may have to handle stress, negotiate and solve problems, accept new challenges and learn how to get along with others. As they conquer new challenges, they build up confidence. Success breeds success. Before you know it, using their repertoire of skills becomes second nature.

There are numerous activities, experiences and short courses that will help give teenagers a head start in life. Challenges should be *fun*, *achievable* (to some degree) and *appeal* to your teenager.

The adventure scale

Although every teenager is unique, it can be helpful to divide them into two broad groups: 'out there' and more conservative teenagers. Your teenager may not fit neatly into one group. However, knowing where your teenager is on the 'adventure scale' helps you to identify extra-curricular activities that will appeal to and challenge them. It doesn't matter what activities teenagers engage in, provided they can gain a sense of accomplishment and pride in doing them. So where is your teenager on the 'adventure scale'? Take a look at Table 5.1 to find out.

Table 5.1 The adventure scale

The 'out there' pack	The 'more conservative' pack
Extroverted ('Pick me!')	Introverted ('Please don't pick me')
Loud ('Here comes Toni!')	Generally quiet ('Where's Toni?')
Resilient	Insecure—need greater resilience
Optimistic	Less optimistic

continued . . .

The 'out there' pack	The 'more conservative' pack
Thrill-seeking (dream of being the new Indiana Jones—want a whip for their next birthday!)	Conservative—don't seek adventure (think Indiana Jones is a nut case)
Confident—love a challenge	Anxious or uneasy in unfamiliar social settings
Social animals ('Let's party!')	Perfectly happy in their own company
Strong interpersonal skills	Prefer to be in the company of close friends and family

Activities for the 'out there' pack

Some people enjoy thrill-seeking pursuits more than others and thrive on the adrenalin rush. Teenagers are infamous for high risk-taking, often romanticising it. Sometimes, providing teenagers with legal and relatively safe opportunities to get their adrenalin rushes can make them less likely to seek excitement in such things as fast cars, fast sex and quick-fix drugs.

Look for:

- fun-packed, energetic activities—from sports like white-water rafting to street theatre or go-kart racing;
- opportunities for leadership, coaching or mentoring others. Learning to take responsibility for others can be a grounding experience for highly adventurous teenagers. Most relish the opportunity to encourage and assist other teenagers and often this brings home to them the importance of safety for themselves too;
- part-time work;
- competitive activities.

If you are worried about your teenager's inclination towards high risk-taking, many health professionals reassure us that it is a healthy and normal part of growing up. Several interesting books containing interviews with teenagers highlight the potentially positive outcomes of teenage risk-taking, if accompanied by appropriate parental and school guidance (see Recommended Reading at the end of this book.)

So what activities suit 'out there' teenagers? The following are some suggestions.

Work/volunteer/exchange programs

The schemes below are recognised worldwide. They allow teenagers to move outside their comfort zone, to work or study with other young people from all over the world. Going overseas has enormous benefits for teenagers. It develops their confidence, broadens their perspective and they return having achieved something they can be proud of.

There are a number of high school exchange programs that allow students to complete several months, a semester or a year in a school overseas. Some of these are:

- EF High School Year.
- Student exchange programs.
- GAP Activity Projects: Students aged 17 to 20 can complete an overseas placement in a variety of countries in various work settings.
- CCUSA: Full-time students aged 18 to 29 can complete paid work experience in the United States for up to five months. They can work in a wide variety of jobs or become counsellors in summer camps.
- Camp America: Students who are 18 can apply. There is no upper age limit.
- STA Volunteer and Work Abroad Schemes: Australian students aged 17 and above are placed in countries in Asia, Africa and the Middle East.
- Raleigh International: Young people from 17 to 25 can volunteer to work on exciting environmental and community projects around the world.
- Investigate other opportunities in your own country on the internet or at school.

Madeleine Shaw, 17

I was so scared before going on exchange. I was thinking, 'What happens if I make no friends?' or 'What if people don't like me?' But when you step off the plane at your destination, you know you've just taken the biggest step of your life. It was awesome. It definitely made me more confident and outgoing—a better person altogether.

School seems so different now. Before I went away I didn't work very hard. Now I want to get good grades. My whole life is so different. I talk to people more, I'm more cheerful and people say they notice a change in my attitude. It's a great feeling being complimented on how much you've changed.

Steve Pask, 25

GAP changed my life. I worked with visually impaired kids in Kent, in the United Kingdom, for twelve months after finishing school. One of my best mates there grew up in the Bosnian war and had been blind since birth because they put too much oxygen in his incubator. As a teenager, he narrowly escaped death when a bomb landed on his house, spraying shrapnel all over him. A year later he was walking down the street with his best mate when his mate was shot and killed. His family then moved to England as refugees. If I ever thought I was having a bad day, he would quickly remind me what a bad day was all about. At the age of 18, meeting someone like this puts your life into perspective and changes the way you view the world. I probably have another 50 stories about people like this who impacted on my life that year.

The GAP experience changed my life professionally too. I have worked as an IT consultant, in pharmaceutical sales and am now the marketing manager at GAP. Every time I have had a job interview I have been asked about my GAP year. They all find it fascinating. I have never failed a job interview. For me, GAP was a way to challenge myself, gain independence, discover the world and widen my perspectives. It was so much more than a year away. It was the best year of my life.

Challenging clubs and camps

These activities are character-building and 'outdoorsy' teenagers love them:

- Army, Navy and Air Force Cadets.
- Outward Bound: Some courses are for young people while others are for families or father–son adventures.
- Scouts.

Peter Garrett AM, singer and social activist, politician

Scouting gave me as much responsibility as I could handle. It didn't set any limits on my desire for adventure. I remember we built a raft and tried to sail it from the Central Coast down to Sydney. We didn't get far but it was an incredible adventure and gave me a lot of self-esteem. Scouting really instils a sense of your own capabilities and gives you a chance to overcome your fears and insecurities.

Chris Lyons, 17

Army Cadets is one of the greatest things I've done so far in my life. Every Monday night I'm focused and ready for anything thrown at me. You feel really important in whatever role you have and feel part of a team working towards a goal. But the most fun things are the bivouacs (camps) three times a year. You get to camp out in the freezing bush, eat rations and get up at 5.30 every morning in nothing but a t-shirt and jocks. I can't imagine a better way to spend the week. The activities are awesome, especially putting on camouflage paint and capturing the flag. It's so much fun.

Activites for the 'more conservative' pack

Teenagers who are more conservative tend to enjoy more passive pursuits. However, I have known many reserved teenagers who have relished challenges like going on student exchange programs and developed greater confidence, *once they got there*. The trick is to encourage them to take that step.

The point is *not* to achieve a personality 'makeover' for less 'out there' teenagers. More conservative teenagers may never enjoy thrill-seeking activities or getting up in front of hundreds of people. But they can increase their confidence to the point where they become more comfortable in large and formal settings. Each time teenagers experience a sense of success, they widen their sphere of comfort and ability to interact with others.

There is a growing tendency for overly shy teenagers to form internet 'friendships' and immerse themselves in a virtual world. This can make tertiary life or life in the workforce more difficult initially for these teenagers. Encourage your teenager to occasionally switch off their computer and find activities they enjoy which involve some social contact with other teenagers.

'More conservative' teenagers should look for:

◎ generally non-competitive activities;
◎ well-structured, well-organised activities where there is a sense of security;
◎ activities that reinforce existing talents so that confidence is increased;
◎ activities shared with small groups of peers. It's always easier for less confident teenagers to mix with people who enjoy similar interests or who are intent on achieving a particular goal.

So what activities suit the 'more conservative' pack? Here are some suggestions.

Individual pursuits

Some students have special hobbies, like model-making, reading, skateboarding, doing weights or web page design. Praising achievements and showing your interest can boost your teenager's confidence and encourage them to try other pursuits.

Part-time work

Even solo activities like paper rounds will enhance self-esteem and lead to other jobs involving more contact with people. Simple jobs in cafes or supermarkets are often where many teenagers taste 'real' responsibility for the first time; it's somehow different from being trusted by parents and teachers. I've seen many teenagers literally glow with pride when you catch sight of them at their part-time job.

Short courses

Short courses such as those at university summer schools and in community centres can complement special hobbies or introduce new interests. These are relatively inexpensive and can be completed in school holidays. Non-competitive and self-paced activities, such as furniture-making, bicycle maintenance or photography, are great. For teenagers who have no special interests, these introductory experiences can open up a whole new world. They are also an excellent way to help teenagers gain the skills and confidence needed to obtain part-time employment. Once again, success breeds success.

Membership of clubs and organisations

There are many clubs centred around special interests, including: sports, book and political clubs, youth groups and computer swapmeets. It's difficult for shy teenagers to attend alone. Perhaps you could suggest your teenager attends with a friend.

Public-speaking courses

Once teenagers have gained more confidence, these can be an 'icing-on-the-cake' experience. One shy student I knew took the big step of completing a public-speaking course, overcame his fear of answering questions in class and giving class presentations, and went on to be a class captain.

Using teenagers' interests to enhance success

The most likely way of finding activities to boost your teenager's 'feel good' factor is to look at their existing interests. Remember that teenagers with similar interests may wish to express them in very different ways. A shy teenager may love science but initially not want to join an environmental clean-up group. They may, however, enjoy reading scientific magazines and visiting science displays and museums. At a later date, they may be ready to join a 'Rescue the Penguins Society' or 'Save Our Creek' crusade. Vastly different activities can give teenagers the same skills and satisfaction.

Here are a few ideas to set you thinking. Does your teenager love any of the following?

The outdoors, science or the environment

- ◉ Visit museums and science fairs with them.
- ◉ Investigate the cost of subscriptions to specialised magazines in these areas. Can they be borrowed from local libraries? Are there websites?
- ◉ Locate voluntary work with conservation authorities and groups.

Animals

- ◉ There are animal rescue societies in many urban and rural areas.
- ◉ Voluntary work can often be undertaken in animal shelters and hospitals.

Reading, writing or the media

- ◉ Look for book clubs, writing workshops, talks by visiting writers and writing competitions for young people.
- ◉ Some radio stations have voluntary work or are run by young people.
- ◉ Some local councils have youth magazines produced by teenagers.
- ◉ The internet now offers many literary competitions and publishing opportunities.

History, current affairs or politics

- ◉ Obtain information about membership of political parties for young people.
- ◉ Book clubs are often of interest to these students.
- ◉ Birthday presents can be good opportunities to give teenagers their own subscription to a newspaper or magazine.

Sports

- Lucky you! There are many great sports clubs and activities around.
- Coaching is another great way to enhance confidence and leadership skills.

Art or music

- There are many art and craft classes around—pottery, jewellery-making, life drawing, Chinese brush painting, calligraphy or photography.
- Students who don't play a musical instrument can always join a choir.
- There are opportunities to help backstage, manage ticket sales or make props for amateur musical productions. These are great social and educational experiences for teenagers.

Jessica Healy, 19

Getting involved in a political party meant that, when I was passionate about an issue or policy, I had an outlet for my energy and could identify with a group of like-minded people. Because the political party I joined respected and fostered the participation of young people, I felt accepted and listened to and I felt good about the skills and opinions I had to offer the party. I was able to become a state-level spokesperson, a state election candidate, and the lead senate candidate for my state in a federal election—all before turning 20. Exploring my political beliefs gave me a broader, bigger picture of the world. Instead of my school environment being my mini-universe, I could see school as an environment that was part of a larger context. There is often too much pressure on students to get good marks. Being involved in things outside school can give you a more mature and less stressed perspective on schoolwork and marks.

Tania Nanuan, 17

I joined the Air Force Cadets two years ago. I guess I joined to finally get something on my CV. Today I continue to go because it has given me lifelong friends and some great skills. I can interact with people of all ages and ranks and I've learnt discipline, stamina and confidence. I've completed courses like Service Knowledge, Aircraft Recognition, Aviation and Fire Arms Safety and have participated in activities such as skydiving, abseiling and orienteering. My involvement in state and national events has given me connections with people all around the country.

While all of the skills, attributes and attitudes are valuable, the most important are *confidence* and *resilience*. They're like the two sides of a coin. Confidence gives teenagers the courage to accept new challenges; resilience gives them the strength to go on when the going gets tough. Teenagers who have both gain more from school and life.

Building confidence

Confident teenagers have a huge advantage because they generally find it easier to improve their skills in most other areas. They are willing to have a go.

How does confidence affect school?

It affects a teenager's ability to form friendships, participate in school activities, give class talks and presentations, to approach exams and generally enjoy school.

How can parents help teenagers develop confidence?

Encourage your teenager to try new activities and take small steps *outside* their comfort zone. The secret is to help teenagers find what they enjoy doing.

- Recognise and praise all achievements even those that have nothing to do with school. Confidence gained elsewhere generally flows over into school.
- Teenagers need opportunities to demonstrate responsibility. But make sure these are achievable tasks.
- Allow your teenager to make decisions. Demonstrating your trust will increase their pride and confidence.
- Allow them to make mistakes and learn from them.

Tommy Rollinson, 14

When I was about 7, mum encouraged me to try dancing and I loved it. She never pressured me to keep going. It was always my decision. Dancing is now very important to me. I have fantastic experiences like competing at state and national levels and representing my country internationally in Dancesport competitions. Dancing and performing have changed me incredibly. Dancing gives me something to dream about and be excited about besides schoolwork. The biggest thing I've learnt is how to act in the spotlight. Many people mistake me for being older because I can mingle with almost any age group. I've learnt how to aim for something and see the bigger picture. I couldn't have done any of it without my mum's support.

Pauline Razos, 15

I started singing professionally in my second year at high school. I've performed at various cafes, at talent quests and sung at school assemblies. Being good at performing is great because I'm achieving out of school and have something to say. Friends support me and understand if I'm busy. I also have friends out of school and we understand each other because we are going through things together. I love seeing the crowd's sense of enjoyment and once I'm on the stage I don't want to get off. It's made me more confident and I can socialise easily with people. It's a perfect way to get rid of your 'bad days'.

Amy Boughen, 17

I applied to be Environment Captain at my school because I care about the environment but also because I hate talking in front of people. With this position I am overcoming this fear. Babysitting has also given me more confidence. I love the responsibility and the fact that the children respect me so much that they feel they can tell me anything. It's more like being a big sister than a job. The responsibility is so amazing and rewarding. I would do it even if I weren't paid.

FAQ: Despite being a high achiever, our daughter is very shy. How can we help her gain more confidence?

A: It's important to talk to teenagers about their fears. Showing empathy and concern is the first and most important step. Be positive. Explain that feeling shy is common and there are ways to address it. Having a plan of action is empowering. Suggest activities listed above for 'more conservative' teenagers, as the answer may be in taking measured 'risks' such as enrolling in a short course where there will be teenagers with similar interests. Allow her to select activities she feels more comfortable with.

Volunteering is often particularly helpful for shy teenagers. Teenagers enjoy feeling needed and there are many community organisations that welcome help. Professionals in these organisations are often tuned into the needs of young people, instinctively recognise those needing a confidence boost and know how to motivate them.

Don't forget how valuable part-time work can be. An extremely high achiever once told me that he had never really felt good about himself until he started to work in a supermarket. Straight As generally aren't enough to make a teenager happy. Working can dramatically increase a teenager's self-esteem, giving them a sense of pride and independence. For shy teenagers, working can be a 'turnaround' experience. The same applies to angry, rebellious or 'disconnected' teenagers.

Tell your daughter that there is no quick solution to being shy but she will gain confidence gradually through life experience. If you see no improvement after a reasonable time, suggest that she sees an experienced counsellor or psychologist. Without help, shy teenagers can withdraw into themselves and sometimes develop social anxiety.

Catherine Madigan, psychologist

The impact of social anxiety on a student's life can be limited to one or two situations or extend to virtually all areas: participating in class, playing sport, interacting with the opposite sex, socialising with peers and dealing with teachers. In severe cases, students may refuse to attend school altogether. I have met people who have said they chose all their subjects so as to avoid or minimise having to do presentations. Social anxiety can influence one's choice of subjects and tertiary course, preventing students from making optimal career choices. Left untreated, adolescents may decide to self-medicate with drugs and/or alcohol and may also develop depression or other psychological disorders.

Building resilience

Things inevitably go wrong in our lives. The ability to get back up and go on is an invaluable skill—especially for teenagers who are often vulnerable and self-critical. When teenagers feel helpless in a particular situation, many respond with anger and self-destructive behaviour. Others shut themselves away and can become depressed. Depression is serious at any age, but for teenagers—who are generally less well equipped to handle its debilitating effects—it's a burden that is sometimes too heavy to carry.[2] Resilience helps protect teenagers from both depression and suicide (see Chapter 8 for signs of depression and strategies to support teenagers suffering from this and other serious issues).

How does resilience affect school?

Enormously. At some point, most students receive a disappointing result or report. Sometimes a single piece of work undermines a student's confidence. Problems with friendships can undermine social confidence. Students who give up when facing setbacks are disadvantaged. As they approach the senior years at school, tertiary education and employment, teenagers increasingly need the ability to handle pressure and bounce back from setbacks and disappointments.

How can parents help teenagers develop resilience?

Teach them that they have power over their lives. Teenagers need to hear over and over again that they have the ability to make decisions and to *change the direction of their lives*. There is always a positive choice, regardless of how tough a situation may be.

Don't overprotect them. Resilience is something we develop through experiences of falling and getting back up on our own. It's difficult to resist the urge to rush in and pick teenagers up, but they won't learn how strong they are unless given the chance to test their own strength. Sometimes teenagers will need parents right there from the beginning while at other times they will be able to cope alone. When in doubt, stand back and give your teenager a chance to go it alone before offering support.

Teach them to be optimistic. Having a positive outlook is a huge advantage for students. They are more successful in all aspects of their lives. Show your teenager that having a 'glass half full' mentality is a learnable skill that simply takes practice. *Optimism is the soul of resilience.*

Teach them to be determined and persistent. Students need determination to handle the challenges of senior study, relationship issues and other day-to-day hurdles. Instil in them a 'don't give up' mentality. Use relevant examples of other young people to illustrate that there are few overnight successes in life—most performers on high-profile TV talent searches have spent years tirelessly training and honing their skills. And if the crunch comes and they have to accept defeat, they can be proud they did their best.

Tell your teenager that strength of character is built on how we deal with setbacks, not how we deal with successes. It's easy to feel good about ourselves when we are successful. It's when we fail and pick ourselves up again that we really show the stuff we are made of. Make sure your teenager understands that the real winners are those who have a never-say-die attitude even in tough times.

Teach them to let go of the past. When teenagers see how parents handle tough issues, they'll learn how to respond with optimism rather than with anger, resentment or resignation.

Teach them that, while some situations cannot be changed, *they can choose their reactions to these*. Young people need to hear that sometimes all we can do is accept a situation no matter how sad or disappointing, and move on with our life.

Good messages to give teenagers about setbacks/disappointment

- Sometimes you can't see solutions alone. Getting advice is the smart thing to do!
- Don't give up! There is almost always a solution to every problem, sometimes many. Talk about personal experiences or those of your own parents or grandparents. Hearing how family

members overcame obstacles is often enlightening for teenagers. All families have great stories to share.

◎ Everyone makes mistakes, has doubts and is occasionally afraid—even parents! This is a good way to reduce pressure to be perfect. You're showing that adults are human too and teenagers don't have to act tough or be perfect to be 'grown up'. Reassure your teenager they don't have to prove themselves or change themselves for you. You love them *as they are*.

Fall seven times, stand up eight.
—Japanese proverb

FAQs

Q: We believe our daughter's social life is preventing her from doing her best at school. Should we insist that she give up these distractions?

A: It's always a risky business to force teenagers to do anything unless the situation is life-threatening or really driving you crazy. Forcing your daughter to give up the activities could be counterproductive; her results might drop even further if she is resentful and angry. A better approach is to discuss your concerns. Show you are proud of her enthusiasm but also believe her education is important. Would she consider easing up on the activities?

Encourage her to think about the importance of school by making her aware of the exciting careers that revolve around her interests. If she's sports mad, she may like a career in sports management, coaching, human movement, PE teaching or physiotherapy for which she must do well in certain subjects.

Some students, however, are not prepared to cut back on their interests for school. They're having *fun* and are not ready for serious study. Sometimes the only solution is to be patient and continue encouraging them to think of future courses and careers. Students often begin studying more seriously when they find something they want to achieve. Support your daughter with her interests and in return ask her to do some career investigation and think about the future a little more.

Q: My son isn't interested in anything apart from computer games. He wastes hours playing games and reading computer books. His results at school are only average apart from IT. What can I do about this?

A: Showing interest in a teenager's abilities and talents is often the best way to establish 'contact' with them. Ask your son to teach you the games. Try beating him (good luck!). Once on the same wavelength, you're in with a chance to discuss more serious issues. Once again, can you build on these interests? Are there computer swap meets you can take him to? Has he considered careers in the IT industry? Investigate these with him. Visit tertiary institutes to speak to lecturers. You *don't* have to wait for Open Days. Lecturers are always happy to meet interested students and parents. When teenagers find courses that interest them, they are generally more motivated to study.

Q: Our son is 16 and has never had a part-time job. All of his friends work, but he says he isn't interested. We believe part of the reason is that he is shy. What's the best approach?

A: A good approach is to discuss the advantages of obtaining part-time work (see Chapter 10). It is, however, difficult for shy students to even apply for jobs, let alone envisage interacting with other staff or the public. But for these students, landing a job does wonders for their confidence. Most students love working, develop a good circle of friends and come out of their shells.

Help by looking through local papers to find part-time positions and share your own experiences of work. Help them prepare a CV and outline qualities and skills relevant to the job they are applying for. Talk to them about the importance of first impressions and discuss appropriate dress and ways to impress employers, such as shaking hands and showing a willingness to learn.

It's important to acknowledge that landing a job is difficult but not impossible. This lessens the disappointment if the first application is unsuccessful. Supermarkets and fast food chains are always a good place to start. Staff members are generally young and the atmosphere isn't oppressive. Delivering newspapers and advertising literature is still a good entry point into the world of work for many young people and is ideal for teenagers who lack confidence.

Q: My 15-year-old daughter appears to be happy at school and at home but she doesn't have any real interests apart from reading. She also spends a lot of time alone. Should we be worried?

A: The real question is whether she is in fact happy. Many parents never *ask* teenagers this question. Ask your daughter whether everything is okay and tell her that she can talk to you about anything. This will reassure her that you are there for her and that may be enough. Some teenagers love reading and can spend hours happily 'lost' in books—I was one of them. Has she always liked reading and spending time alone or is this new? If it's a sudden change, make sure she really is happy and isn't covering up a problem in her social life. Try introducing her to new interests by getting information about clubs, societies and short courses that would appeal to teenagers who read.

It might help to call a counsellor at the school or a teacher who knows your daughter well and ask them if they have noticed whether she is mixing happily with peers. Does she have at least one good friend? It would be a concern if she has no friends.

There is no quick answer to this situation. Your daughter could be perfectly happy or hiding the fact that she is being bullied at school or is worried about exams. Be observant, spend time together and reassure her that you are there for her, whatever her concern.

In essence

Encouraging teenagers to undertake activities often gives them the skills and self-confidence to make the most of school and life beyond school. Encourage your teenager to live life to the full knowing that you will be there to help them on their way if they occasionally trip up.

> *Life is a great big canvas, and you should throw all the paint on it you can.*
>
> —Danny Kaye

6 ✣

Study and school skills

All our dreams can come true...if we have the courage to pursue them.

—Walt Disney

I have seen hundreds of students who could have enjoyed school more (and who could often have been more successful academically) if they had developed a more positive and proactive approach to their studies. Many also lacked practical strategies to make studying easier. You can help your teenager 'skill up' and 'motivate up' in vital areas such as:

- ◉ developing a positive attitude to school;
- ◉ understanding and utilising their preferred learning style;
- ◉ organising and handling study and homework;
- ◉ goal-setting and achievement;
- ◉ time management.

This is not a 'How to Study' guide. There are many excellent texts available for students and you could recommend these to your teenager (see Recommended Reading). This chapter provides suggestions on how parents can help teenagers *help themselves*. You are like the coach working to motivate the players before a big game. They are the ones who have to play the game. But you can provide those invaluable messages to encourage them and help them take responsibility. Strategies to help your teenager follow.

Developing a positive attitude to school

While your first urge may be to chain them to the books and bolt the door to their room, resist it . . . it's illegal. There are other more subtle ways to achieve your objective:

- Help them de-stress. Students who are under enormous stress to obtain high scores often cannot relax enough to concentrate. Make sure your teenager isn't living under the impression that you expect perfect scores. Teenagers must identify ways to relax during times of high stress (see Chapter 10).
  Parental pearl of wisdom: 'Just do your best.'
- Get them information. Make sure they're aware of all of the advantages of doing their best at school and know about the many exciting pathways that school opens up for them.
  Parental pearl of wisdom: 'Have you seen this fantastic new course/article/career?'
- Treat their 'day job' seriously. Teenagers respond well when adults recognise their efforts. Acknowledge that you know school can be a hard slog, but there's no getting around it.
  Parental pearl of wisdom: 'It's not easy, but it's worth it.'
- Help them to develop the right mindset and a strong mental attitude. Encourage them to understand the work rather than simply memorise it. Encourage your teenager to take control and proactively seek out help by approaching teachers, reading study guides or attending study seminars.
  Parental pearl of wisdom: 'When the going gets tough, the tough get going. There are many ways to make studies easier . . .'
- Help them prioritise. Students often need help organising their time and commitments. Those with no outlets for relaxation easily become tired and stressed, while too many distractions can adversely affect studies. Having a good balance not only allows them healthy outlets, but also encourages them to apply time management skills to the real world.
  Parental pearl of wisdom: 'What do you want to achieve? What do you need to do to get there?'
- Offer constant encouragement and support. Kids need a pat on the back when they perform well. Tell them how proud you are and they'll go the extra mile. The power of positive reinforcement will amaze you.
  Parental pearl of wisdom: 'Well done!'

Louise Yeomans, principal

Parents need to ensure their teenager has a balance of school, outside work and leisure. It's not easy being the parent of a teenager, but parents need to maintain their standards and stand firm against unreasonable requests from teenagers.

FAQ: My son takes lots of breaks during study time and final exams are approaching. Are breaks really necessary?

A: Absolutely . . . provided they don't occur too frequently. Students should take five- to ten-minute breaks every hour. This allows them to relax and return to study recharged and alert. Some students tell me that their parents comment every time they leave their room: 'Shouldn't you be studying?' This diminishes any possible relaxation and doesn't demonstrate trust. Resist the temptation to ask. If you notice he has been tempted to sit down in front of the TV when you suspect he has work to do, make your comments casual: 'How are things going?' or 'Much more work to get through tonight?' Ultimately, teenagers have to take responsibility. You can provide the support, the place, the materials and the food; they must supply the commitment.

Understanding and utilising their preferred learning style

People learn differently.[1] Teenagers can study more effectively when they utilise their preferred learning style. It helps them understand their learning rather than just memorising. It also means less work for the same outcome!

Investigating the preferred learning styles of all family members is interesting and can make school seem more important. It becomes challenging and *fun*, rather than a deadly serious 'let's discover how you'll get better results' quest. Here are a few facts and strategies to suggest to your teenager:

- *Visual learners* enjoy reading, drawing maps and diagrams and watching movies. *They learn well by seeing.* Encourage your teenager to use mind maps and other visual summaries of topics rather than simply reading and taking lengthy notes. Explain that drawing diagrams and maps may help to recall knowledge during exams. Identify visual resources to increase their enjoyment of topics being studied: movies, documentaries, internet sites or illustrated texts.

- *Auditory learners* are less likely to enjoy reading. They prefer to *discuss* ideas, to question *and* ask. Encourage your teenager to ask questions and participate in class discussions. Encourage them to try explaining difficult topics to you, to talk it through. This often helps students clarify thoughts and increases memory retention. Many students study for exams by going through the major points or issues out loud, sometimes while walking around. I've known many students who have taped themselves explaining topics and concepts out loud and played this back (with headphones) while travelling to and from school. They say it's magic. Some students successfully study with a friend who is also an auditory learner. By explaining issues to each other and discussing problems, they reinforce what they are learning.

- *Kinesthetic learners* or *tactile learners* learn best by physically *doing* things—by *touching* objects or models, by building and making, by participating in real-life activities. Research shows that a high percentage of boys enjoy learning like this rather than by reading and discussing.[2] Kinesthetic learners have difficulty in classes where there are few opportunities to do things. Locate internet sites where students can undertake virtual tours of everything from archaeology sites and art galleries to the anatomy of the human eye. (Visual learners are also in seventh heaven with all of this.) A growing number of exhibitions, art galleries, science and natural history museums have state-of-the-art interactive displays that kinesthetic learners love. Introducing your teenager to these may increase their understanding, curiosity and love of learning.

FAQ: Our son says school is boring, yet when he is fixing his bike, or assembling a complicated electronics kit, he never loses concentration or motivation. How can we optimise this?

A: Your son appears to be a kinesthetic learner who learns through and enjoys hands-on activities. Many schools now have very practical vocational courses in a wide range of areas (see Chapter 9). Are any of these courses at your son's school? If not, investigate other local schools that do offer vocational courses or other programs that may have more practical components. Students like your son often thrive when they incorporate one or more of these courses into their schooling. I've known students who are suddenly willing to concentrate in more traditional school subjects because they can look forward to their vocational classes.

If vocational courses are unavailable in your area, help your son look for part-time work in an area that interests him. Could he work in a bike shop or a workshop where electronics equipment or other components are being repaired? Positive experiences with work may increase his confidence and motivate him to want to do better at school in order to pursue courses and careers in these areas.

Organising and handling study and homework

Good schools only set homework that reinforces what is being taught, helps students clarify ideas or prepare for future classes. Consequently, if teenagers fail to take homework seriously, they generally have difficulty doing well. Here are some tips to encourage your teenager to do homework:

- Provide a homework-friendly setting. While teenagers should pull their weight around the home, it's important that they have adequate time and a quiet place for homework and study. While the entire home shouldn't revolve around homework, you need to ensure other family members aren't blasting music in the next room. Showing you believe homework is important encourages teenagers to take it more seriously.
- Encourage a homework routine. Having fairly regular mealtimes helps enormously. Good planning allows time for other things and homework won't dominate their entire existence.
- Help them to begin. Teenagers often procrastinate. Sometimes gentle encouragement helps them to 'get started' so that they finish sooner and can relax.

- Help them to avoid distractions. Discuss the benefits of discouraging friends from phoning, emailing or SMSing during homework time. Avoid banning friends, as this generally backfires, causing anger and reducing development of self-control and self-motivation. Asking siblings to respect each other's study time also encourages teenagers to feel the work is worthy of special consideration.

- Explain that homework is often about the process rather than what they learn. Homework helps refine important skills they will use in the future: researching, evaluating knowledge and summarising information.

- Encourage your teenager to take responsibility and accept homework. The 'just do it' advice often works. Tell them it's part of life and not to waste energy grumbling. Explain that practice makes study easier each time, as it does with other skills.

- Reward effort. Many students, especially senior students, say how much they appreciate parents bringing them in a snack during their homework/study time. It's also a good opportunity to offer some encouragement: 'Good on you. You'll get the hang of it' or 'Would you like me to read over it?'

- Be involved but don't 'hassle'. Teenagers hate nagging, preaching or anything resembling surveillance. Low-key approaches work best. A casual, 'How's work going?' or 'What are you working on tonight?' is preferable to 'Have you finished your homework?' or 'Shouldn't you be studying?' Whenever possible, stand back and let them learn to stand on their own feet.

- Show genuine interest. Discuss work being covered. This is very different from 'hassling'. Ask: 'What does the assignment require?' 'Do you need a hand getting started?' Offer to proofread work. Look for relevant newspaper articles or TV documentaries on themes and topics. Some students love all of this; others hate it. Play it by ear.

- Evaluate progress. If friends or distractions are constantly interrupting or the homework routine has been ditched, it's time for a heart-to-heart talk. Sometimes we all need a little nudge to keep on track.

Because homework is one of the most hotly debated school issues, here are some of the questions I have heard a million times:

FAQs:

Q: My son is very disorganised and is constantly behind with school-work but he refuses to let me help him. What can I do about this?

A: Many teenagers won't allow family members to help them. It's often part of the 'I don't need you' syndrome. If your son won't discuss organising a timetable or looking at better ways to study, tell him that you want to meet his school counsellor to discuss ways he can catch up. This approach works best if the underlying message to him is, 'There is nothing wrong with you. We might be able to find an easier way for you to approach study. Let's see what your counsellor suggests.'

Approach the interview with the counsellor with sensitivity. It's a 'make or break' affair! Always allow your son to speak for himself and *never* criticise him. 'Loss of face' is a huge issue for teenagers.

Never say: 'X is very disorganised and behind in his work', or 'We've always had trouble getting X to do his homework. Perhaps you can talk some sense into him.' (I've heard these statements many times and the negativity they cause in the students listening isn't pretty.)

Perhaps try something like: 'X has a lot of homework. Could you suggest some effective study techniques so that he has more time left for other things. We don't want him studying all of the time. X, would you like to say how you feel?' This doesn't judge or criticise your son and allows him to talk *if he wants to*.

Q: My daughter is swamped with homework and rarely has time to spend with the family anymore. The school gives her way too much homework. What can I do?

A: Never hesitate to contact a school, but going in with guns blazing makes it difficult to find the best solution for your teenager (see Chapter 8).

Sometimes homework spirals out of control and, unless parents speak up, schools are unaware of what's happening. If the school assures you that your daughter is one of only a few students having difficulty, it's time to discuss ways of supporting her. Does she know how to study effectively or is she in her room procrastinating? Is she coping academically? Does this school cater for her interests? Talking to school staff can sometimes help locate underlying problems. These may have everything or nothing to do with homework.

Q: My son isn't interested in anything except music. He rushes through homework and plays the guitar for hours. How can we get him to be more serious about school?

A: Try turning things around and using his interest to encourage him to study. Identifying courses and careers where a musical talent or interest in music can be utilised may give your son an incentive to study more. I've also known parents who have enrolled their teenagers in summer music camps (science or art camps) with the proviso that they complete the year at school successfully. This is also a great way to help teenagers learn how to work towards a goal. And take heart, you may also have a budding John Lennon or Andrew Lloyd Webber in the house!

Q: How much should we help our daughter with her homework?

A: Helping teenagers with their homework provides bonding opportunities and enables parents to better assess their teenager's abilities. Helping should be just that, however. Though it can be difficult to judge, when you find yourself taking over the keyboard or repeatedly saying to your child: 'Here, let me do it', you know you've crossed the line.

Assist by planning steps, interpreting topics, discussing options, reading over drafts and even getting resources from libraries or the internet. Most of all, show interest and support with simple words of reassurance—'That looks good' or 'Sounds like an interesting topic'. Sometimes, this is all teenagers need.

As a rule of thumb, students should be progressively taking greater responsibility for doing their own work as they move up the school.

Spoon-feeding in the long run teaches
us nothing but the shape of the spoon.
—Edward Morgan Forster

Q: My son insists he can study with loud music playing and also frequent interruptions from friends. Isn't all of this distracting?

A: Although many experts would say that loud music and distractions are generally counterproductive, a mother recently told me that her son did surprisingly well in his final exams despite the loud music and the internet chats. As with all research, there will always be exceptions to the rule, and each student needs to identify as early as possible what works best for them. Help your son to identify his ideal study environment *before* he reaches senior high school or tertiary education. Suggest he tries different study environments. He may be pleasantly surprised by the outcome. Allow him to make the final decision, however, as teenagers must learn to take responsibility and to accept the consequences of their decisions.

Neville Lyngcoln, principal

When parents inquire about homework, the most common responses are 'I don't have any', 'I did it at school' or 'It's not due for another week'. It's pretty unlikely that no homework has been set and 'It's not due yet' is a big red flag. Procrastination is a huge problem for students. Often when they feel overwhelmed, it's because everything has been left to the last minute rather than too much work being set. It's important for students to get into good study patterns before they reach the senior years, where more study of a greater complexity is required. Students also need to understand that planning well and using homework diaries leaves more relaxation time. It's hard to relax when you're worrying about how you'll get your assignment finished. But if you're organised, it's easier to 'flick the switch' into relaxation mode and take a proper break. Parents can help with this. If you're familiar with their schedule and help them plan a homework diary, it will be much easier to be supportive and constructive rather than adding to their pressure.

Goal-setting and achievement

Teenagers with their sights set on a goal, whether this is completing an assignment or reaching a particular level of success, can generally focus more. They have a *reason* to work hard. As students enter senior years, the goals generally become bigger and more important. Knowing how to plan and break a task into *achievable steps* helps teenagers avoid becoming overwhelmed or falling behind. Here are a few tips:

- Help your teenager set realistic short-term goals and break tasks into bite-sized chunks.

- Give them opportunities to taste what it's like to work for something. If everything comes too easy and teenagers never have to strive for anything—even saving for new jeans or making it into the school musical—they will never learn determination and persistence. They will also never know the satisfaction that comes from achieving something on their own. Not doing everything for teenagers isn't being tough, it's allowing them to grow up.
- Offer 'incentives'. Contributing to a savings goal once they have reached a particular target, or planning a special event to celebrate achievements are different from offering 'bribes'. It's putting the responsibility squarely on them but showing you appreciate their hard work and want to reward them.
- When things don't go as planned, help them reassess, set new goals and move forward.

Time management

Students unable to make good use of their time are often behind and rushing through work in the early hours of the morning. Good time management is all about forward planning. Here's what you can do:

- Help your teenager plan a study and homework timetable. Without a plan, neither student nor parent can keep up with what is done or what is due. The plan should be realistic. Allow time for favourite TV programs, sport, friends and special interests.
- Encourage them to backward plan. Knowing when work is due and working backwards is a sensible way to ensure there's sufficient time to complete each task.
- Encourage them to take five- to ten-minute breaks each hour so they remain fresh and able to study effectively. Staying in a room for lengthy periods without breaks is counterproductive. Students hate being reminded about returning to study. Bite your tongue and wait for them to make the move.
- Encourage them to stick to their plan. Planning is useless if it is not followed. Encourage them to be disciplined in sticking to their study timetable. They'll finish their homework more quickly, leaving more time for relaxation.
- Teach them the art of re-evaluation. A timetable may need adjusting

due to unforeseen events or commitments. Some students give up when a timetable doesn't appear to work. Encourage persistence.

In essence

Parents play an invaluable role in supporting teenagers through the 'hard slog' all students must put in to do their best at school. In a real sense you are their motivational 'psychologist', their coach, sounding board, backstop, taxi driver and chef extraordinaire. They couldn't do it as well without you.

Education is . . . hanging around until you've caught on.
—Robert Frost

Part IV

CLOSE ENCOUNTERS OF THE TEENAGE KIND

handling the big issues

7 ❃

Home matters

If a child is to keep his inborn sense of wonder, he needs the companionship of at least one adult who can share it.
                                                        —Rachel Carson

Educational researchers say, 'The home environment is one of the most important factors influencing academic performance.'[1] Everything that happens at home has the potential to either give teenagers a head start and protect them from harmful risk-taking or adversely affect them.[2] Teenagers who are angry or resentful about situations at home often release their pent-up frustrations at school. Teenagers sent to me for counselling are often so angry about home 'stuff' that a career direction and schoolwork are the least of their concerns.

Although many home situations and circumstances may be unpredictable and unavoidable, teenagers who feel loved and accepted unconditionally at home have an invaluable stability in their life. The home environment and parental interactions with teenagers are like the foundation blocks on which they design and build their identity.

Home is where the heart is! Here are some home help ideas that will make schooling a more positive experience for your teen.

Make home a good place to be

Whatever is happening at school, home should be where teenagers can let off steam (sometimes enough to power a small factory), test out opinions and find unconditional acceptance and support. At home, teenagers should feel:

- safe;
- listened to;
- respected;
- trusted;
- important; and
- that you are on their side.

It was Albert Einstein who said: 'Most teachers waste their time by asking questions which are intended to discover what a pupil does not know, whereas the true art of questioning [is] to discover what the pupil knows or is capable of knowing.' As your child's most important teacher, ask them questions—not to discover what they don't know or what they are up to, but to find out what they believe and fear, what their dreams are and how you can help them to realise those dreams.

Common teenage fears

Being afraid to take home results

Some parents hit the roof or instigate restrictions on their teenager's freedom if a particular result or report isn't what was expected.

What can parents do?

Few students enjoy poor results. This is precisely when they most need support rather than reprimanding. A less than impressive result is an opportunity to chat about things and discover ways to help your teenager. Help them pick up and move on. (See the section 'Make school reports count' later in this chapter.)

Believing parents have impossible expectations

This is one of the most difficult situations for teenagers. Associated stress often affects their ability to sleep and concentrate. Silence or a disappointed look can hurt as much as angry words. One of my students put it very well: 'My parents are so intense they scare me. I see it in their eyes. I feel like I'm being watched all the time. It makes me tired just thinking I might disappoint them.'

What can parents do?

When does encouragement to do well become persecution? Ask yourself whether your teenager is already doing their best. Many students say their parents refuse to accept they are trying hard. This is one of the quickest ways to make teenagers dislike school and it may increase stress to the point where they cheat or simply give up.

I'll never forget the desperate student who handed me a downloaded copy of Act 3 of *The Glass Menagerie*—word for word—as his creative writing piece for English! He probably assumed few teachers would have read such an obscure-looking play. Sadly for him, I had. When I casually commented that I thought the plot was a 'tad familiar', he went an eerie shade of white. I hastily added that he could resubmit the work after the weekend. He thanked me profusely and we became firm friends from that point on. When I met this student's father on parent–teacher night, I saw immediately why my student had been pushed to the point of cheating. Although he was a high achiever, his father was unsatisfied with several results.

Many teenagers also misinterpret signals from parents. Sometimes they have the *perception* that their parents have impossible expectations when this is far from the truth. *Tell* your teenager you are more proud of effort than results. Don't assume they know how you feel.

Feeling pressured to do nothing but study, study, study

Students should never have to sacrifice all of their interests, friends and part-time work because of studies. All work and no play rarely produces good school results.

What can parents do?

Every teenager is different, so help your teenager find the right balance between study and a social life. If they are overcommitted socially, encourage them to cut back a little. Let them decide what and how. And if they are overdoing study, remind them that occasionally taking time out is *beneficial*, not a waste of time.

Feeling problems at home make it impossible to concentrate

Students mention that situations such as the following trouble them:

- disharmony between parents/caregivers;
- separation of parents;
- serious or chronic illness of a family member;
- death of a family member;
- inability to see eye to eye with a parent or sibling;
- financial strain;
- unemployment or stressful work situation of a parent;
- moving house/changing school—which often results in the loss of friends.

What can parents do?

These situations all involve some form of loss for teenagers—loss of the family unit or of life as it was. There may be no way to change what's happening at home, but generally it's always best to do the following:

- Tell teenagers what is happening and reassure them as much as possible. Young people who feel loved and trusted are amazingly resilient. Teenagers prefer honesty and detest being left out of things. Parents may believe they are protecting teenagers, but hiding things usually increases stress. Knowing is usually better than wondering and imagining.
- Set the example. Show that life goes on. If teenagers see parents fall apart, they often follow suit.
- If possible, minimise disruption affecting teenagers. Don't let them become entangled in conflict situations.
- Ask your teenager how they feel and what would help them cope better. With all the best intentions, making decisions for teenagers can result in even more distress.

Give your teenager practical support for school

Research shows parental interest in their children's schooling has positive results. One study of 570 000 students found that those whose parents regularly *asked* what had happened at school each day performed better than students lacking this.[3] So don't forget to ask, 'How's school?'

One of many interesting recent studies reveals that certain parental practices enhance student engagement with school and learning.[4] These are:

1. Actively helping to organise and monitor students' time out of school

Helping your teenager organise out of school time is one of the most important things you can do. Students need outside activities to relax and unwind after school.

2. Helping with homework

Issues surrounding homework frequently top parents' list of worst nightmares. See Chapter 6 for an in-depth look at homework issues and strategies to use for common problems.

3. Discussing school with them

School is a huge part of your teenager's life. Know what's happening in it. Being informed enables you to support them and prevent problems.

Great questions to ask about school:

- ◎ Do you like school this year?
- ◎ Is there anything that worries you about school this year?
- ◎ Who is the best teacher you have?
- ◎ What are your favourite subjects?
- ◎ What are the hardest?
- ◎ Is there any way I could help?
- ◎ Do you think I expect too much from you?
- ◎ What would make school better?
- ◎ Is it true a lot of bullying goes on in schools? Have you or your friends ever been hassled?
- ◎ What would you most like to change about school?

Teenagers generally give better answers when questions arise casually in the course of talking about life in general—perhaps at the dinner table or while driving somewhere. The point isn't to investigate but to show your interest in their world so that your teenager will be more inclined to discuss concerns with you. If possible, have a laugh with them about some of the funny things that happen at school.

Be involved in their school

There are many ways to participate:
- parent associations;
- fundraising and social activities;
- school councils;
- working bees;
- information nights and other events.

But don't feel guilty if work and other commitments prevent you from participating in these activities. The most effective way to help your teenager is to show your interest and stay informed about their schooling. You can do this every day in your own home.

Be there as a sounding board

At some point, most teenagers adopt that easily recognisable teenage attitude with a capital A. Ironically, the tough act often hides insecurity. Home should be a safe place where your teenager can experiment with different 'versions' of themselves and have a fling with the hair dye, interesting clothes and personal opinions. If they can't 'break out' at home, it's more likely to happen in inappropriate ways at school. Help your teenager develop the ability to:
- give an opinion without criticising;
- acknowledge alternative viewpoints;
- share their opinions with you without fear of being rejected.

Instil a love of learning

This is an invaluable gift for teenagers. School can nurture it but the seed generally has to be planted at home. This has nothing to do with results and everything to do with helping your teenager appreciate how exciting the discovery of new topics and ideas can be. Many research programs are investigating ways of helping educators not simply to churn out teenagers who have acquired facts, but to produce people who can think for themselves, who are open to new ideas and the acquisition of new skills—people who are able to thrive in our fast moving world. In other words, to prepare young people well for the future, schools have a duty to help them feel positive about learning and open to becoming *lifelong learners.*[5]

Even more than schools, it is parents who can help instil a love of learning in their teenagers through their everyday interactions with them. Help your teenager by:

◎ picking up on casual comments and using these as starting points for conversations on a wide range of topics;
◎ showing interest in issues of concern to them;
◎ asking their opinion on an issue or event.

Make school reports count

I see more students worrying over reports than many other aspects of school. The way parents approach reports can make school a more positive experience for teenagers. See reports as opportunities to reassess what support your teenager requires.

What can parents do?

Regardless of their results, ask your teenager how they feel. They may be happy, proud, upset, angry, disappointed or defensive. Be prepared for all possible reactions and be positive and supportive. 'I think you have a lot of ability and I want to help you any way I can. Let's talk this over.'

Discuss the report honestly but without accusations. Tell them how you feel, but avoid words like 'disappointed', 'let down' or 'I knew this would happen'. Most students already give themselves a hard enough time—they're just good at hiding it.

Help your teenager to identify realistic ways to move forward: studying more effectively before exams, managing time better or fewer interruptions from friends during study time. Sometimes it may even be necessary to discuss changing subjects or looking at alternative schools.

Focus on the positives. There must be something positive in the report! Glowing comments about effort and contribution to classes should be recognised and genuinely praised.

Don't push too hard. Reassure your teenager that you are proud of their efforts and don't expect impossibly high scores.

Never be complacent about the 'wow' reports. Some teenagers, reliable as clockwork, come home with glowing reports that can make your day. But teenagers are sensitive to *everything* parents say to them or *omit* to say. Throwaway questions like '95 . . . what happened to the other 5 per cent?' can make them think parents are not satisfied with their results.

Don't take all comments as gospel. Teachers are not infallible. I've seen many students work like Trojans to prove them wrong . . . and so they have. And some comments are not worth losing sleep over. A teacher once told a parent that her daughter was a 'strange child' whose essays contained 'strange ideas'. She went on to say that *if* she managed to complete high school, she would certainly be struggling to get into university. Thankfully her mother didn't share these comments with her daughter, who blissfully went on to do surprisingly well both at high school and even university. (Thanks mum! The irony was that I loved school and was especially proud of my essays.)

Read between the lines. Don't ignore situations hoping they will go away. Is the teacher saying your teenager is struggling, a real annoyance or a loner? Be proactive and discuss the comments with your teenager and the teachers.

Decoding school reports

- 'Christine is very vocal in class and needs to consider the opinion of other students.'
- *Probably means:* Christine tends to be a big mouth. Tell her to shut up occasionally.

- 'Jack tends to distract those around him in class and would benefit from listening to instructions.'
- *Probably means:* Jack is a pain in the neck and won't do what he is told. Tell Jack he needs to cut out the funny business and listen

to his teacher if he wants to be the millionaire lawyer he keeps saying he wants to be.

◎ 'Sally has worked extremely well this semester but has had difficulty with some of the concepts.'
◎ *Probably means:* Sally is having difficulty with this subject despite working hard. Go easy on Sally, praise her for her efforts and ask if she needs help.

◎ 'Alex could improve his results by completing set homework more thoroughly. Presentation of work needs serious attention.'
◎ *Probably means:* Alex treats homework as a joke. I can't even read his writing. Does Alex always say he has no homework or that he has completed it on the bus?

FAQs

Q: We have some major family issues at the moment that are affecting our son's results at school. Should I contact someone at the school about this?

A: It's important to let someone at your son's school know that he is having a tough time. Casual comments from teachers such as 'Come on Tony, you can do better than this' affect students differently depending on their home situation. As a teacher, I've experienced first-hand how difficult it is to judge when a student needs a push to work harder and when they need space and special consideration. Being aware of home situations allows teachers to offer support—extensions of time for work, accepting (without comment) that the standard of work isn't as high as usual or even granting exemptions from certain assignments. All of this can be done without alerting other members of the class to what is happening so that confidentiality is maintained.

Ask your son whether he would like to speak to the school counsellor alone. Sometimes teenagers will speak more freely to someone who is not directly involved, and this can help release a lot of stress.

Q: What can you do when teenagers refuse to discuss school?

A: If they seem to be happy, relax. But occasionally ask questions and stay informed about what is happening as much as possible—even if you only get one-word answers. Teenagers often go through stages when they don't want to talk to parents about *anything*.

If the refusal to discuss school is sudden and dramatic, however, this could indicate an underlying problem—perhaps bullying or friendship issues. Dialogue isn't a one-way street, so occasionally break the ice by talking about your day and funny or interesting incidents. Your teenager may then open up and share information with you. When teenagers continue to clam up about school, it might be wise to discuss this with a school counsellor.

Q: My daughter is doing okay at school but she could do better. How can you judge how much to push kids when it comes to doing well at school?
A: Getting the balance right is a fine art. And what may have worked with your teenager a few years back, even a few months back, may now upset them. Everyone has different 'drivers'. Some teenagers respond well to encouragement, praise or gentle reminders while others need frequent reminders or even a shove in the right direction. Some shut down completely when they feel they're being pushed at all. It's like judging how much to water a very touchy indoor plant. Tread carefully and observe the effects of various approaches. Teenagers are generally good at telling parents when they need space. When you notice an approach that works, remember it and use it again. Eventually you'll discover what works best.

Q: I'm worried because I don't believe I can help my son with his studies any more. Everything is so different to when I went to school. What can I do?
A: This is a common concern for parents, especially as their teenagers enter the senior years at school. The reassuring news is that you don't have to be able to understand the actual work your teenager is studying. Just being there for them and showing your interest is invaluable. Even keeping the food and drinks flowing can be a pick-me-up for teenagers. One student told me that during stressful times his mother would bake him a chocolate cake. 'Mum doesn't say anything but when I smell that cake cooking, I know she understands I'm a bit swamped with work. It's kinda nice. It makes me smile.'

Q: My daughter's school reports are becoming more and more difficult to interpret. What can I do?
A: Never hesitate to contact the school to discuss terminology and comments. Schools should *welcome* questions and concerns. Provided

you approach with a smile on your face rather than folded arms and a scowl, you should be able to sort out exactly what the report is saying and not saying. And you have every right to expect a smile and a professional approach from the school.

Here's proof that the home fire never dies:

Jo Hamer, parent

Memories of childhood often involve doing things together as a family. As our children progressed through the years, we deliberately did things together to create a bond of shared experiences. We tried to 'be there and be involved' and share our children's interests. My husband has been a leader at Cubs, Scouts and football. I've done the committee thing and helped out with school clubs in which our kids have been leaders.

And then, along came archery! Initially, Rohan, then 12, wanted to take it up. In our usual style, my husband did the course as well to make it a special father–son time. They got the bug. Rohan, who up to this stage had not found something he was good at, discovered he had a natural talent for archery. Within six months, he was competing successfully at state level. Our other children, then 14, and 10, became interested. At this stage we were spending two to three hours most weekends in each other's company sharing something we all enjoyed.

While we still have individual interests, archery is a family thing. We have been able to stand next to each other and compete on an even basis. As archery is not dependent on size, age or strength, the children can easily match or beat adults. It's been fantastic. It's provided:

◎ regular time as a family;
◎ an opportunity for all of us to feel special and good at something (we have all competed at state and national level);
◎ a goal to work toward and experience doing one's best;
◎ the experience of dealing with disappointments and being generous and gracious in success and defeat;

- an opportunity to give back and develop leadership skills—Rohan, Dean and Roy all run coaching classes and are qualified coaches;
- an opportunity to gain recognition regardless of age, size or sex.

Archery has had a huge impact on our family. It has contributed to our individual sense of worth and resilience while enhancing a strong sense of family. We continue to look for opportunities to share things as a family—family relationships are important and we want them to be strong and real.

Keep it burning.

Nine tenths of education is encouragement
—Anatole France

8

What else is happening at school?

When a teacher calls a boy by his entire name it means trouble.
—Mark Twain

Many teenagers breeze through school with few dramas—they make good friends, do well in their studies, cope with maturing sexually and stay well balanced throughout. Others struggle with all or some of these aspects of growing up. Whatever issues your teenager may face, being well informed will enable you to support them.

Understanding undercurrents at school

It isn't just what happens in the classroom that affects a teenager's ability to do well at school. Indeed, it's often what happens outside school hours and hidden from your sight that dramatically affects progress. It's also what often keeps parents worried at night—those nightmares about teenagers being caught up in:

- high risk-taking;
- eating disorders;
- sex;
- drugs;
- depression and even suicide.

Before looking at warning signs for these, let's examine what could lead there: the influences affecting a teenager's ability to succeed and be happy at school.

School is so much more than a place where teenagers study. It's where teenagers learn to socialise with others and find themselves. It's a microcosm of society. It's often where they will first fall head over heels in love. It's also where they can fall victim to peer pressure to engage in the nightmarish areas parents dread.

Sometimes when teenagers don't show the enthusiasm we'd like for school, we assume that it's somehow related to studies. Often they're simply more interested in or preoccupied with everything that's happening to them. School often can't compete with first dates, the first kiss, a fight with the best friend and other events teenagers consider life-shattering. Teen hormones, emotions and the working out of identity and values can sometimes wreak havoc. At this age, school life *is* real life. All that happens at school—the friendship groups, the parties and the occasional schoolwork—is pretty much their entire world.

It's vital that parents help teenagers negotiate their way through the undercurrents at school. Crucial areas to examine are:

- friends;
- peers/peer pressure;
- relationships;
- sex and questioning sexuality.

Your teenager's ability to handle each of these areas will affect their self-esteem, their ability to do well at school and their ability to avoid being caught up in dangerous areas such as drugs, eating disorders and other high risk-taking activities.

The role of friends

Teenagers with no friends at school can rarely be happy and do their best. Having friends is different to being accepted by peers. Don't be concerned if your teenager is not the most popular student. Having even one good friend can be enough to make teenagers feel comfortable at school. If you believe your teenager has no friends at all, it's important to discuss this with a school counsellor. Teenagers need friends.

Tony Frizza, principal

I have made it a practice for many years to arrange a meeting of youngsters and their families in the year prior to their coming to high school. One of my standard early questions is, 'What do you like best about school?' The most frequent response by a very long way is, 'My friends'. Having close, long-term, caring friends at high school is clearly the most important factor in a youngster's enjoyment of it, or otherwise. Genuine friendship will lead to happiness and enjoyment, even when some other important factors are either missing or present only intermittently.

Jackie Yowell, parent

I used to worry that Jake would generally have only one or two good friends at a time. This meant that if the friends were away, or they had had a blue, Jake was alone. But eventually I accepted this was his preferred pattern of friendship, with all its risks. These days, being more mature, he balances his friendships more evenly between close and more distant friends. I also accept that he will never be a 'herd' animal, enjoying big groups or gangs, but always preferring fewer, closer friends. A mother's lesson!

Helping teenagers negotiate the friendship storms

No magic recipe can help teenagers find good friends at school, but there are some strategies worth trying:

- ⊚ Encourage your teenager to take opportunities to make new friends such as participating in school clubs where they can meet like-minded souls.
- ⊚ Many students also strike up friendships with fellow students on public transport to and from school, so encourage this.
- ⊚ Talk to them about how to get along with others by being proactive and making the effort to start conversations. Help them further develop confidence by participation in out-of-school activities (see Chapter 5).

- Having contact with similar-aged cousins or children of family friends can lead to new friendships.
- Suggest they invite other students home.

FAQs

Q: My daughter's reports are no longer up to her usual standard and she doesn't appear to care. I blame her friends, who monopolise her time. Should I ban them from contacting her during the week?

A: Only if you want to drive your daughter *away* from you. Friends are sacrosanct! Approach reverently. Focus on your concern about her results. Ask her how *she* feels about the reports. What does *she* want for the future? Encourage her to take study more seriously by helping her investigate careers in line with her interests. Ultimately, it must be teenagers themselves who decide they want to put in the required work at school. Parents can only help by offering sensitive guidance (see 'Lacking focus or motivation for study' in Chapter 9).

Q: Our son is 16 and wants to spend a lot of time alone. He doesn't even see friends out of school much at all. Is this normal?

A: Teenagers frequently need their own space away from parents, so if your son suddenly wants to be alone for lengthy periods, this doesn't necessarily indicate trouble. But it's important that he continues to participate in family activities such as mealtimes. This enables *you* to keep in touch with how he is feeling and what is happening in his life. Generally teenagers snap out of this pattern after a while.

Cutting contact with friends, however, could be more of a concern and it's vital to see why this change has occurred. *Teenagers need peer contact and affirmation.* Some teenagers chat incessantly about friends while others never mention them unless asked. If you believe your son is increasingly isolating himself from friends, contact a school counsellor and investigate why.

Q: Our daughter wants to move schools because her best friend is moving to another school. This is impossible—it's located across town. What can we do?

A: Sympathise! For a teenager, having a best friend leave their school is traumatic. At no other period in our lives are friends so crucial as in the teenage years, so don't suggest that there will be other friends. Acknowledge that this is a difficult time and support her through it. Explain that it's impossible for her to move to the new school because of the distance, but discuss practical ways she can maintain contact with her friend. Can they see each other on weekends and holidays? Most teenagers need time to get over losing a friend at school, so be patient with her.

Q: How can parents encourage teenagers to form positive friendship groups rather than getting in with a bad crowd?

A: Tactfully! Criticising friends often makes them more attractive or drives teenagers closer to them on principle! Teenagers listen to parents more when their pride doesn't get in the way. If you say anything, give your opinion in a non-judgemental way. 'Jason's so lucky to have a friend like you helping him with his assignments.' This is so much more effective than blurting out that Jason is a user.

How peers and peer pressure can affect school

Teenagers *crave* acceptance by their peers, so issues relating to peers can significantly affect their happiness at school. Peers provide a visible measure of whether they are okay or not, so passing the test to fit in is a terrifying ordeal. Teenagers go to extraordinary lengths to please their peers, and negative behaviour at school is often the result of wanting to be seen as 'cool' and part of the 'in crowd'. Wanting to fit in can also induce some teenagers to develop poor body image, eating disorders, depression and even suicide if they feel unacceptable to their peers.

Adolescence is also a time of experimentation, discovery and blind confidence. Peer pressure combined with curiosity and a feeling of being invincible leads many teenagers into activities that give parents sleepless nights. Sometimes you wish you could keep teenagers at home, safe from harm— but they must learn to stand on their own feet and make wise decisions when you are not there to protect them.

FAQ: How can parents help their teenager fit in with peers at school?

A: No teenager should feel obliged to change themselves, act in any way they feel uncomfortable or hide anything about themselves in order to fit in. This is easy to say, but monumentally difficult for teenagers who crave acceptance. The best way parents can help teenagers, especially if they are 'different' in any way, is to build up their self-esteem. Help them to see their unique talents.

First of all, teenagers must know parents accept them 100 per cent. Teenagers who feel unacceptable in their own homes are doubly disadvantaged. Helping them find like-minded peers—even out of school—is the next important step (see activities listed in Chapter 5). Finding acceptance anywhere generally increases a teenager's self-esteem, making them less vulnerable at school. Sometimes it reverses the downward emotional spiral some enter, and as they gain more confidence they also begin making friends at school. Teenagers smell confidence as quickly as insecurity and fear. Some teenagers may never be part of the most popular group, but often this is a blessing in disguise. Popular groups aren't always the most admirable souls.

How to protect teenagers from peer pressure

- Praise your teenager's qualities and achievements. Teenagers with high self-esteem are less likely to succumb to peer pressure.
- Talk to your teenager about the dangers of peer pressure. Tell them that it takes more strength of character to stand up for their beliefs than blindly following the crowd. Add that you do realise this isn't easy.
- Help your teenager to fit in as much as possible so that they don't become a visible target for peers to criticise. We've all heard the saying 'kids can be cruel'. Wherever possible, allow your teenager to participate in peer activities. The student who is not allowed to go on the school camp or attend the end of year celebration can be singled out for ribbing from peers. These students often seek to prove they are 'cool' by engaging in high-risk activities.

Relationships and their effect on school

When the first girlfriend/boyfriend appears on the scene, tread carefully. Teenagers are highly sensitive to any criticism of the 'love of their life'. Making them welcome in your home gives you an opportunity to know them better and see more of your own teenager.

It's important to know that there is a high level of pressure on today's teenagers to have a boyfriend/girlfriend and even begin a sexual relationship. In my health classes recently, a student made an interesting comment: 'If you don't get a girlfriend and do stuff, they call you a frigid or say you're a freak and stuff.'

To help teenagers with relationship issues, parents must impress on teenagers what they should expect in all relationships:

- respect—no pressure to act in ways that make them feel uncomfortable and the ability to say 'no';
- the ability to be themselves;
- support and encouragement;
- honesty;
- feeling safe.

Talk to your teenager about the importance of being safe and not finding themselves in the wrong place at the wrong time. Teenagers need parental advice and guidance as they develop their own beliefs and sense of morality. At the same time, it's important to validate teenagers' feelings and recognise that they are growing up and want increasing levels of freedom. Teenagers must learn how to handle responsibility and make the right choices themselves. Many complain that parents simply say, 'You'll get over it. You're too young to have a boyfriend/girlfriend anyway'. Such comments produce hurt and anger and are not conducive to concentrating on studies.

FAQs

Q: Our son would like to have a more lively social life but is painfully shy, especially with the opposite sex. How can we help him?

A: Most teenagers grow out of this, given time, but there are a few strategies that may speed up the process. Encourage your son to take up an activity such as a short course where he may meet girls who share his interests. (See activities and confidence building strategies outlined in Chapter 5.) Is there someone he would feel comfortable talking to—an older cousin, an uncle or family friend he relates well to? Ask this person to find an opportunity to casually chat to your son about his social life. He also needs reassurance that it is common for teenagers to feel shy around the opposite sex. It may help him to know that many girls also feel equally shy. If you feel able to chat with your son, perhaps even share some of your own fears at his age.

Q: Our 16-year-old daughter seems to be obsessed with boys, sexy clothes and parties. How can we get her mind back on school?

A: Your daughter sounds like a normal 16-year-old. While it is important not to criticise her interests, talk openly about your expectations. Teenagers need to know the values their parents hold. They want to be recognised as 'grown up' so this is a good opportunity to mention that balancing fun and studies is a sign of maturity. Say that you believe she has enough maturity to realise that her future is important. I've also known many parents successfully enforce the house rule that school-work is completed *before* their teenagers go out with friends.

Sex and questioning sexuality

If you're secretly hoping your teenager hasn't started to think about sex much, think again. The next time you leave the house, take a look around you. Everything from billboards to the words of your teenager's favourite songs contains sexually explicit material. Marketing seduces hormonally charged teenagers at every turn. Here is some background information to consider:

Facts about teenage sex/sexuality and what they mean for parents

- A recent study shows that approximately 48 per cent of teenagers have had sexual intercourse by the time they reach their final year of high school.[1]
- Providing teenagers with sex education and opportunities to discuss relationships delays them becoming sexually active. It also enhances self-esteem, and allows them to be more responsible, better informed and able to protect themselves, resulting in fewer unplanned pregnancies.[2]
- Twenty-five per cent of teenagers who regularly use the internet often have unwanted exposures to sexual images. Seventy-four per cent of these teenagers believe that public concern is warranted and think adults should be 'extremely concerned'.[3]
- Knowledge about sexually transmitted infections (STIs) remains poor.[4]
- Approximately one-quarter of all sexually active students report having had unwanted sex at some point. Most cited being too drunk and peer pressure as reasons for this.[5]

It's obvious that, while teenagers often appear to be very sophisticated and knowledgeable in all matters, they do need guidance in making wise decisions regarding sexuality. Is your teenager aware that pressure to begin a sexual relationship is unacceptable? It is concerning that many students report having unwanted sex. Teenagers are often not good at thinking situations through, and can find themselves in unsafe situations. Discuss issues of safety. Talk openly at home about the potential consequences of unwise decisions.

Many teenagers are misinformed about this area, especially if they are relying on what friends *think* is correct. Although most schools have sex education and the need to initiate a sit-down 'birds and bees talk' disappeared long ago, understanding input from parents is probably the best way for teenagers to learn about sexual relationships. It is also important for teenagers to know the values that are important to their parents. Although they may sometimes appear not to, teenagers generally do listen to parents—especially when issues are discussed openly and in a supportive manner.

Parents who feel uncomfortable discussing these issues don't have to pull up a chair and launch into a 'let's talk about you-know-what' session. Informal chats are often less embarrassing for teenagers (and parents) and can be more effective. Opportunities often arise during popular teenage television programs. Just happen to be around during the episode where Tina is deciding whether to have sex or where Jason is being lured into an unsavoury relationship. It's much easier to ask, 'So what do you think about what Tina/Jason chose to do?' than to start a conversation out of the blue.

Helping teenagers as they question sexuality

While there is plenty of lively discussion about sex in high school health classes, a less discussed issue is sexuality. Few schools are free of homophobia, and peer pressure to conform and have a girlfriend/boyfriend is significant and affects all students—regardless of their sexuality. Today's teenagers often *question* their sexuality earlier than previous generations because they are generally more sexually aware.[6] Between 8 and 10 per cent of young people are attracted to the same sex[7] and as many as one in four teenagers question their sexuality, many finding this a frightening experience—especially if they believe their parents are negative about homosexuality.[8] As most teenagers are too shy to broach this subject, it is important to find an opportunity to casually reassure them that you are not homophobic. With greater visibility of gay characters on TV, this isn't too difficult to do. Give your teenager the clear message that your love and acceptance are not conditional on them being heterosexual.

It's important to know whether your teenager's school has clear policies to address homophobia and whether these policies are then acted upon. All students should be safe at school, regardless of sexual orientation.

Same-sex oriented youth are:

- often aware of their sexual orientation at an *earlier* age than previous generations due to increased visibility of gay issues. However, they still face great difficulty in forming a positive sense of self and identity due to high levels of homophobia and silence surrounding this issue in schools;[9]
- frequently victims of verbal abuse and even physical assault (one study revealed that 50 per cent experienced verbal abuse and 13 per cent physical assault—most of which occurred *at school*);[10]
- more likely to turn to alcohol, drugs,[11] and suffer from depression;[12]
- more likely to attempt suicide.[13]

Anthony, 19

Sexuality was scary to figure out even though my parents are the most supportive I know. In high school, anyone who doesn't fit the mould is terrorised and tormented. I have friends who can't be open about their sexuality with their parents. This is a shame as it means they don't know who their children are. Friends of mine have had to sever all ties with their parents who would rather not have their children in their life if they 'choose' to be gay. I cannot understand this. These mates of mine have had to find a new family in their friends. This can be great but it's not the same. I can't understand how this feels, as I have never had to deal with it. I guess I'm lucky.

FAQ: Our son has many female friends but he's never had a girlfriend. We're starting to suspect that he might be gay. What should we do about this?

A: Your son may simply not be ready for a girlfriend. However, in case he is gay, make sure he knows how you feel about this issue. If he is gay and knows you are *not* negative about this, he will talk to you when he is ready.

Unfortunately, many parents are afraid to discuss this topic, believing that talking will encourage their teenager to become gay. Talking to teenagers about sexuality *will not make them gay*. It could, however, spare them untold misery. Teenagers who are afraid to come out as being gay to peers and family are doubly isolated. Remembering that 8–10 per cent of young people are attracted to the same sex, it is important to be informed about this area so that you can support your teenager. A teenager's life and happiness will not be compromised should they be gay *provided they feel loved and accepted by those who matter most in their life—parents and family.* There is always a certain level of apprehension associated with 'coming out'. In compiling and editing *Inside Out*, a collection of autobiographical stories from the Australian gay community, some of the unhappiest young people I have ever encountered were those who feared rejection by parents because of their sexuality. Tragically, many were contemplating leaving home, were suffering from high levels of stress, depression and were self-harming and suicidal. Make sure your teenager feels safe and loved *unconditionally*.

Identifying when your teenager is at risk

Remember those nightmares that keep you awake at night: drugs, sex, depression and suicide? Sometimes the only way you will know whether your teenager is becoming caught up in high risk-taking is to be observant. *Never assume changes are simply 'teenage stuff'*. Hormones may be the reason, but look for underlying issues.

Identifying changes in behaviour—especially if *sudden, dramatic and seemingly without cause*—can sometimes help you catch teenagers before they fall. Here are some of the most common warning signs to look out for:

Signs of depression and drug taking:

◎ moodiness, and noticeable personality change;

- feeling unmotivated, lacking energy;
- withdrawal from social contact;
- loss of interest in activities and other previously enjoyed aspects of life;
- inability to sleep or sleeping longer than usual;
- staying home from school/work;
- declining school/work results;
- changes in eating patterns—gaining or losing weight;
- noticeable physical deterioration—tiredness, headaches, minor illnesses, headache;
- impaired memory and concentration.

Additional signs of depression:

- taking unnecessary risks;
- being negative about everything.

Additional signs of drug taking:

- untidy appearance, disorganisation;
- suddenly developing new friends;
- unwillingness to bring friends home;
- sudden need for more money;
- money and items of value disappearing from home.

Signs of suicidal tendencies

Factors listed for depression and . . .
- drawing pictures or writing about death and dying;
- talking about wishing they were dead, or saying people would be better off without them;
- giving away personal possessions;
- self-harming;
- suddenly and inexplicably happy or elated after a lengthy period of being very depressed.

Signs of eating disorders:

- withdrawal from social contact;
- decreased interest in hobbies;

- preoccupation with appearance, weight, dieting and food;
- reduced concentration, memory;
- moodiness, anxiety or depression;
- anxiety around mealtimes, skipping meals and making excuses not to eat;
- trips to the bathroom after eating;
- suddenly wearing baggy clothes;
- obsession with exercising;
- weight loss or fluctuating weight;
- fatigue, faintness, bowel problems and other physical problems.

These are the most common signs. For detailed information on the differences between bulimia and anorexia, contact support and counselling services in your area.

What to do if you suspect your teenager is at risk

- Don't go into that 'great Egyptian river'—denial. Pretending it might go away is wasting valuable time.
- Do lots of reading about the issue you believe may be affecting your teenager so that you can speak confidently to them. Don't hesitate to pick up the phone and ask for information and advice from support services.
- Confront your teenager and talk. Be calm, try not to cry and above all be reassuring.
- Don't blame them or say, 'How could you do this to me/yourself/ us?' Teenagers tell me these are commonly heard words.
- Reassure your teenager that nothing could make you reject them. This may encourage them to tell you what is going on.
- Have literature ready to give your teenager to read. While teenagers are infamous for believing they are invincible, in reality many are shocked to learn the negative effects of drugs and eating disorders.
- If your teenager denies being on drugs or in trouble of any kind, don't jump back into that famous river. Most teenagers initially deny being in trouble. Give them some space but go back for another talk, especially if you notice the warning signs are still present. A persistent but gentle approach works best.

- Be vigilant. Teenagers are great at concealing things, particularly when they know parents are watchful.
- If your fears are verified, convince them to accept help.
- If they refuse, get that special person in their life to talk to them—it's essential to get help as soon as possible.
- Don't blame yourself—these things happen to the best of us and you must be strong to help your teenager.
- Make sure you have someone you can offload to.
- Above all, don't panic. There are many people and organisations to contact for support.

Where to find help for the tough times

Some of the best sources of support you may consider are:

At the school

There must be someone at their school with whom they *connect*, someone who knows your teenager well enough to be able to approach them tactfully and get them to talk about what is happening.

Subject teachers

If it's parent-teacher time, identify which teacher is most pleased with your teenager's work or praises their efforts. Trust this teacher and tell them you are worried something is upsetting your teenager. Teachers are generally observant and can also find opportunities when students may talk about personal or academic issues.

Welfare staff

If no subject teacher springs to mind, there are generally great welfare staff and counsellors in schools. Sometimes year level coordinators also handle welfare issues.

Other staff

Sometimes students 'connect' with the school photocopy person, the nurse or a librarian. Once alerted to your concerns, a member of the welfare staff or a level coordinator can pick up on these important connections. They can then approach this person and ask them to encourage your teenager to talk about school.

Out of school

Sometimes people outside school know your teenager well—perhaps the coach of a sports team or the parent of a friend. Often a grandparent or another relative can be encouraged to talk with your teenager and inquire how things are going.

Outside counselling

If all your detective work reveals nothing but you still believe that something is *not right* about your teenager, seek a professional opinion—from your family doctor, a youth worker/ social worker or a psychologist. There are many government-sponsored and private organisations offering support for teenagers and their parents confronting issues such as eating disorders and drugs. Many parents have told me they were afraid to seek advice as they felt they had failed as parents. Counsellors and support staff are non-judgmental and extremely understanding. Children of even the best parents can encounter problems.

The role of school staff

Friends, peer pressure and relationships are important, but teachers are important too. Teenagers who can establish positive relationships with teachers generally have a happier time at school. There are some practical ways parents can help teenagers negotiate issues that may arise in their dealings with adults at school.

The most common complaints about school from teens are issues surrounding:
⊚ teaching quality;
⊚ discipline;
⊚ managing conflict with staff.

What can parents do?

Discourage the 'us and them' mentality

Unfortunately, many teenagers believe that all adults, including teachers, are out to get them. Dispelling this myth can save teenagers unnecessary angst. Encourage your teenager to see teachers as people who are there to help them. Encourage them to speak to teachers when difficulties arise rather than waiting until they are behind in their work. If the work is too easy, teachers welcome students who take the initiative to ask for additional reading or topics to investigate.

Encourage teenagers to adopt an accepting attitude to school rules

The most common conflicts between students and schools generally revolve around school rules. Tell your teenager that following rules shows maturity and will also save them valuable time spent in detentions. While most people would agree that a 'tuck your shirt in' rule isn't as important as a 'don't swear at a teacher' rule, in some schools neither rule is negotiable. Discuss this issue at home so that your teenager can live more graciously with school rules. Explain that even workplaces have some code of conduct—staff rules and expectations.

Accustom teenagers to having clear boundaries

While teenagers *hate* to be told what to do, ironically they like to *know where they stand*. They must learn to accept that some lines cannot be crossed, despite the fact that they may disagree with them. Schools play a part in the moral education of young people, but parental influence is irreplaceable. Having some rules and clear expectations at home makes it easier for teenagers to abide by school rules.

Encourage teenagers to think before speaking

If every request by teachers is met with 'Why?' or 'What for?' teenagers find themselves rather unpopular. I've often witnessed teenagers digging themselves further and further into trouble as their anger escalates. The good old, 'Count to ten! Think before you open your mouth and blow it!' is still good advice. Advise your teenager to walk away and calm down before approaching difficult situations.

Model how to respect others and apologise

Knowing how to resolve interpersonal conflicts helps defuse situations that often distract teenagers from studies and enjoying life. Teenagers need encouragement to approach teachers and peers to apologise and resolve conflicts. On numerous occasions I have counselled students who were in hot water at school for various reasons. Many are surprised when I suggest they apologise. 'Teachers won't listen to students', they say. Occasionally I have helped students draft letters of apology when they were afraid to approach a teacher or coordinator in person. Help your teenager in situations like this. Tell them that teachers and other adults are *impressed* when teenagers have the maturity to apologise.

FAQs

Q: Our daughter says her maths teacher is hopeless and her friends agree. What should I do?

A: It's important to define 'hopeless' with teenagers. For some, it's a teacher who won't allow constant chatting in class. The important question is whether this teacher is doing their job. There will invariably be teachers your daughter will like more than others. She may even 'hate' some. It is unlikely that there are many completely 'hopeless' teachers in schools today.

Sometimes students find it difficult to adjust to different teaching styles each year. Has your daughter given herself time to adjust to this teacher? Can she approach them and tactfully say she is finding the work difficult? This may help the teacher know your daughter more and see that she is interested in passing. I've seen this work very effectively.

We must also acknowledge that sometimes (if rarely) the teenager is *not* paranoid and the teacher is 'hopeless'. One student I know complained for several years about his maths teacher. After a few weeks with a new teacher, his results improved dramatically and he is now studying maths at university. If parents really believe there may be an issue with a teacher's ability to teach, they should approach the teacher and outline the difficulties their teenager is having in the subject. If this is unsuccessful, discuss the issue with a school counsellor. This should only be done, however, after thoroughly discussing the issue with their teenager to ascertain that there is not a personality clash or other factors at play.

Q: My son doesn't like his history teacher and is often in trouble with him. He used to enjoy history, but now wants to drop it. What should we do?

A: Teachers do make a big difference to a student's enjoyment of school and results. Once again, a teacher and student can simply experience a clash of personalities and this is a good learning experience for teenagers. Ask your son to be open with you about why he dislikes the teacher. Can he overlook these factors and simply see this teacher as someone who is there to provide what he needs to complete history successfully? Explain that it's not common for students to like all their teachers. That's life. But this shouldn't prevent him from doing well if he is determined enough. It would be a pity for him to lose out by dropping history over one teacher, and chances are he won't have the same teacher two years in a row. It's also important to ask your son to honestly think about whether he has contributed to the conflict with his teacher. Why is he in trouble with this teacher? Can he avoid this so that he can focus more on the subject?

How parents can interact positively with school

There may also be times when you feel it's necessary to approach your teenager's school in order to support them through difficult times, or even through conflict situations with school staff. Knowing how to best approach the school can make an enormous difference to the outcome.

Many parents tell me they are reluctant to approach schools even over minor matters, let alone when they believe disciplinary action taken by the school or other issues affecting their teenager are unacceptable. *You should feel comfortable and confident about approaching your teenager's school.* Here are some strategies to make the process easier:

Be fully informed

Never approach a school without first thoroughly discussing everything with your teenager. Knee-jerk reactions often backfire. Be clear about whether your teenager is even partly to blame before approaching anyone.

Always reassure your teenager that you are on their side and that nothing they might tell you would change this—and nothing should. Tell them you must know *everything* that has happened in order to help them. You need to know the worst! I've attended many interviews where it is clear that the teenagers are afraid to tell their parents the whole truth.

Work together with the school

Research shows that when parents and schools work together students benefit.[14] If you see school as the enemy, this will be communicated to your teenager, who may find it hard to respect people you openly criticise. Schools should similarly welcome parental requests to talk about concerns. A good school will openly admit if they have failed your teenager in any way and be willing to look for positive ways forward.

Approach is everything

There are three main styles commonly adopted by parents when approaching schools. Some styles have more positive outcomes for teenagers than others.

The rabbit approach

These parents are intimidated by schools and reluctant to voice their concerns. They are afraid to question school procedures even when believing the school is at fault and hop out of sight when challenged. This disadvantages students as it eliminates opportunities to work with the school to solve issues.

Don't be intimidated by schools. After all, you are 'the client'! It's your right to express concerns. If you are concerned, however, approach school welfare staff. They are generally supportive and can advise you on how to address your concerns.

John Flanagan, principal

Parents should avoid reacting too hastily or dramatically to anything that happens with regard to their child's schooling. A knee-jerk response to a concern could have the effect of dissuading a child from sharing information with parents in the future and could also mean approaching the school 'with all guns blazing' without being aware of all the facts. This is not to suggest that parents should do nothing. They certainly should share any concerns with the school, especially if they become aware of a serious matter.

The bull approach

These parents see school as the enemy and charge in, nostrils flared. It's bad for your blood pressure and isn't going to endear you to the school staff your teenager has to interact with every day. By avoiding accusations and attributing blame, you maximise your chances of a positive outcome for your teenager.

The owl approach

These parents are the wisest of all. They are assertive and approach school positively but firmly. This gives parents the greatest chance of resolving issues. Another wise and effective strategy is to also relay good news stories to teachers rather than only approaching when problems occur. Teachers often comment that compliments from parents are rare. Thank your teenager's teachers for looking after them. If your teenager has been encouraged and inspired by a particular teacher, let them know how much you appreciate this. Telling a teacher your teenager thinks the world of them is a great way to strengthen relationships between teachers and your teenager.

Tony Frizza, principal

Parents should never forget that they are the child's first teachers . . . that it is the role of the school to complement the work of the home. Open, honest and frank communication with the school can assist the school to provide the best environment for the child. It is going to be difficult for the child to enjoy high school if all they hear from home is a litany of complaints, criticisms or objections to what the school is trying to do. Parents are in an important partnership with the school in leading their children to an independent and fulfilling adulthood.

FAQs

Q: I think my daughter's teacher has punished her too harshly for her behaviour in class. What can I do about this?

A: If your daughter's school is notorious for strict discipline, it's pointless to jump up and down. Student diaries often outline school rules or you can obtain a copy from the school website or the general office. Is the teacher simply following school policy? If so, you have a difficult road ahead. In most schools, rules are rules. If the rules are unreasonable, contact the school to discuss your feelings. Rules can sometimes be altered when schools are aware of how parents feel. If no one says anything, rules remain unchanged.

Another important question to ask your daughter is why she was misbehaving in the first place. What did she say or do in class? Can she avoid repeating this in future? Can she see the teacher's point of view? There is another 'lesson' teenagers can learn from these situations. We all sometimes find ourselves in situations where we don't agree with the necessity for or rationale behind a particular rule, but go along with it because, quite frankly, we have more important things to think about and bigger battles to fight! I often tell students that tucking in their shirts won't kill them. Discuss this with your daughter. Is the battle really worth fighting? If it is, support her through it.

Q: Our son was very upset with the comments from one of his teachers. What should we do?

A: Approach the school calmly and explain your son's feelings. It's always advisable to contact the teacher in question rather than approaching their superiors. We all appreciate the opportunity to explain our words and actions. The teacher may be completely unaware that your son is upset and merely be trying to encourage him to work a little harder. Most teachers do care about students and would be concerned if their comments had upset a student. Give the teacher an opportunity to explain their comments and also to understand how your son feels. Problems like this can generally be sorted out with open and honest dialogue. If, however, you are unhappy with the response from a teacher, don't hesitate to contact the level coordinator or the school administration.

Q: We are horrified to learn that our son has been caught cheating. We have been contacted and have an appointment to see his coordinator. How should we handle this?

A: It's important to discover why your son has cheated. Is he behind with work or struggling to understand it? Some teenagers cheat 'for the hell of it' and to impress friends. But I've seen more students cheat because they desperately wanted to please parents than for any other reason. Teenagers can misread messages. Does your son feel you expect more than he can deliver? Quietly point out that cheating is cheating and that it's never the right thing to do. Teenagers need to know that parents have beliefs and values that are important to them.

It's essential to support your son in the presence of the coordinator, to explain you have discussed what has happened and that it won't happen again. I frequently advise students to take the initiative and apologise rather than waiting for teachers to request this. A sincere apology from a teenager is very impressive. However, if the school wishes to enforce some punishment, your son should willingly accept it. *Taking the consequences on the chin is a great learning experience for teenagers.* Above all, make sure your son knows that the incident is over and he can move on. I've had more students than I care to remember tell me that they have given up trying because parents or teachers have never let them forget one 'stuff up'.

Every saint has a past and every sinner has a future.
—Oscar Wilde

Q: I've tried negotiating in a reasonable manner with my daughter's school over several issues but I'm not happy with the response. Who can I contact for help?

A: If you have exhausted all avenues at the school, and the outcomes are unsatisfactory, go higher. Contact the Department of Education in your state and ask for assistance in solving the dispute. Do this only as a last resort, as it isn't going to win you friends at the school. Even if you discover that the school is in the wrong, life for your teenager may be difficult when there is ongoing tension between the school and yourself.

While I strongly believe that sometimes schools get it wrong, ultimately what is most important is your teenager's happiness. It may be wise to look for another school with policies you and your teenager can happily support.

In essence

Being well informed about the danger areas and difficulties teenagers can encounter allows you to be there when they most need you. There is a solution to every problem.

Parents can only give good advice or put them on the right paths, but the final forming of a person's character lies in their own hands.

—Anne Frank

Chapter

9

Hot spots at school

Always take an emergency leisurely.

—Chinese proverb

Previous chapters outlined ways in which you can help make your teenager's home life and general school life better. Beyond general schooling, however, there are some common danger areas teenagers may confront. This chapter provides practical strategies for you to use to help your teenager avoid these. These are the times when parental determination and resourcefulness can help teenagers keep on track or find their way back if they have lost focus in any way.

Some of the big black school holes teenagers can fall into are:

- bullying (as victim or perpetrator);
- lacking focus or motivation for study;
- 'failing';
- wanting to leave school early.

These are danger areas for teenagers because they often have a make-or-break impact on their schooling and a lasting impact on their self-esteem.

Bullying

Being bullied is one of the most destructive experiences teenagers can have. Unfortunately, it's a common problem in most schools. Bullying is the number four reason why young people seek help from the Kids' Help Line and the call frequency is rising.[1] Never under-estimate the destructive effects of bullying.[2] It can cause teenagers to hate school, damage their self-esteem, and affect their ability to sleep, eat, socialise and generally be happy about life. Bullying should *never* be ignored. At its most extreme, it can lead to depression and even suicide.

Some indicators of bullying

◎ Does your teenager appear to be constantly tired? Upset? Moody?
◎ Do they avoid talking about school?
◎ Do they seek opportunities to avoid going to school?
◎ Do they suddenly find excuses to be driven to school?
◎ Have eating patterns changed? Are they constantly suffering from minor illnesses or fluctuations in weight?
◎ Do they avoid spending time with the family and friends?

Who is bullied?

Generally, teenagers who are perceived as being different in any way—overweight, tall or short for their age, short-sighted, for instance —are often targets of bullying. Unfortunately, no student is safe, although those who have a healthy self-esteem are generally more protected from bullying.

Some reasons why teenagers are bullied:

◎ ethnicity;
◎ resisting pressure to behave in a certain way;
◎ high achievement;
◎ new at school;
◎ sexual orientation;
◎ disability;
◎ socio-economic background;
◎ low self-esteem.[3]

What can parents do?

- Show empathy—never trivialise or dismiss what the teenager is experiencing. 'These things happen' are not words that give any comfort.
- Encourage your teenager to talk about what is happening. If no action is taken, bullying generally continues. Bullies often don't expect their victims to tell anyone or do anything.
- Reassure your teenager that they are not to blame and that bullying is unacceptable.
- Talk to them about peer pressure and make sure they are not being forced into behaviour they are unhappy about. Can they avoid some situations? Can they make other friends?
- Discuss ways to be assertive rather than passive or aggressive.
- Help them devise strategies to confront the issue. These could be to stand up to the bully or have a few responses up their sleeve.[4]
- Teenagers who want to study in a school where it is not 'cool' to achieve are in an unenviable situation and can become the brunt of jokes. Likewise, students in a school where achieving highly is commonplace may feel stressed if they cannot 'measure up'. Teenagers in this situation will need support; sometimes the only solution is to consider another school.
- If your teenager is the new kid at school, give them lots of support during this period and keep an eye out for signs they are not settling in because of bullying.
- Teenagers who are being bullied because peers believe or suspect they are gay need to know they are safe at home and not in danger of being rejected even there. I have counselled many students whose school results were suffering because they were worried about rejection from parents over their sexuality (see Chapter 8).
- If you discover your teenager is being bullied, contact a welfare person at the school immediately. Even one supportive person at school can make a difference. Schools do have policies to address bullying, but these tend to be enforced more at some schools than at others. I have known students who have left a school where they felt unsafe and then thrived at a new school where the students were more accepting and staff made a concerted effort to ensure bullying was virtually non-existent. How does your teenager's school handle bullying?

Elaine, 14

I did talk to mum about the bullying but not at the beginning. Not till it got really, really bad. I thought it would go away. At the end I just didn't want to go to school anymore because I was being attacked in the corridors every day. Emotionally I felt better after telling mum because I got it off my chest. I didn't have it stuck in my head all the time. The last time things got bad, I went to the school counsellor. The bullies were very angry with that. They were saying, 'She can't do that!'

Mum's perspective . . . Cathy

Elaine was always a happy child. She loved school. Suddenly she was so unhappy, grumpy—quick to tears. There was obviously something going on. Eventually it all came out. She was being verbally and physically abused, tripped, shoved, even received death threats through the net. She was distraught. She'd come home so upset she couldn't even do her homework. She was exhausted every day. So after school I'd let her unwind then I'd ask her what had occurred that day. We'd work out strategies together—what to say, what not to say, what to do, how to cope. We discussed it every day.

David, 22

Being good at music and theatre, reading books without pictures, being fat and wearing bad glasses tends not to attract friends and acclaim. I had a few friends at school but they were sometimes in the same boat as me! Not exactly an army to fight back with. The best part about it is, after you leave school, you meet a few more people like you (get better glasses or contacts!) and you start being appreciated for the very things people didn't like you for at school. What got me through high school? Parents who told me I was better than the people who were tormenting me. I also had two amazing teachers and no matter how hard anyone tried, they wouldn't allow me to feel bad about being me.

FAQ: We don't think our daughter is being bullied but we've heard that you sometimes can't tell it's happening. How can we know for certain that she isn't being bullied at school?

A: Unfortunately you can't always tell if a teenager is being bullied despite actively looking for clues. Many young people feel ashamed about being bullied and suffer in silence unless someone brings up the subject with them. Say something like: 'We've heard that there are awful bullies at school—are there any that bother you or your friends?' You will generally be able to gauge from a teenager's reaction if they are affected. Talking can greatly relieve stress for anyone being bullied. There are some fantastic books on this area (see Recommended Reading).

What if your teenager is the bully?

Teenagers who bully are generally unhappy and need support. Teenagers commonly bully:

- to get power;
- as a way to be popular or get attention;
- to scare others and hide the fact they are scared;
- to take out their unhappiness on others;
- to retaliate when they are being bullied themselves;
- to fit in when they fear being isolated.[5]

If you discover that your teenager is bullying others, identify what is making them unhappy enough to act this way. Speak to counsellors at their school, and seek professional advice outside the school if needed.

Lacking focus or motivation for study

This is one of the most common laments from parents, regardless of whether their teenager is getting marks of 5 or 95. 'He's not trying hard enough!', 'She never studies', 'He's much more capable than this', 'She's away with the fairies' . . . Sound familiar? It's natural for parents to want their teenagers to do their best at school.

It may comfort you to know that, for most teenagers, losing study focus is a phase. There are strategies parents can use to help teenagers refocus and see school in a more positive light. If you think your teenager is not performing at their best, you can probably spot which study profile they fit:

The happy cruisers

These teenagers are quite happy to coast along, putting in the minimum effort. They pass, sometimes even quite well, but could do so much better. Some of them are having a great time at school—veritable social butterflies! Probably one of the most common report comments is, 'Sam could do better by listening in class, participating in discussions, and generally working with greater effort' (read: Sam doesn't even bother faking interest).

The hormonally affected

These teenagers lose focus for a time and have an 'off year'. Often the only reasonable explanation appears to be raging teenage hormones.

The bored

These teenagers see school as boring or irrelevant. 'This is a waste of time', 'Why do we have to learn this stuff?' Sound familiar?

The 'not school ready' bunch

These teenagers don't do well at school or show any interest in studies. As victims of late developers syndrome, they simply don't 'get it all together' in time to do their best in high school. The good news is that, *provided their self-esteem is kept intact*, these teenagers often return to study a few years down the track, enjoy it and experience success. The difference I have seen in students given time to mature is remarkable. Sometimes late bloomers become the high flyers of tomorrow.

However, those who are constantly told they are lazy, dumb or 'not academic' take much longer to regain the confidence to return to study—if they ever do. Don't allow a few 'off' years to irreparably damage your teenager's self-esteem. Nothing is more precious.

The 'horrible friends' afflicted

Sometimes peer pressure can be disastrous for teenagers. The pressure *not* to perform well can derail many previously good students. Boys are particularly susceptible. Around middle high school, it sometimes becomes 'nerdy, uncool and sucky' for boys to study and (God forbid) get good marks.

Teenagers can also fall into the groove of 'mucking around' at school, and peers expect them to be loyal to the gang and continue this behaviour. Going against this pressure is extremely difficult. Some students make the wise decision to change schools and make a fresh start where they are not expected to be really good at being really 'bad'.

Billy Hannah, 17

I used to answer back at school and not listen. I got into heaps of trouble because I'd tune out and do the opposite to what I was told. I hated being told what to do. In classes I sometimes felt it was my job to make people laugh. I was a bit of a clown. Everyone in the cool group mucked around. I had fun. I was The Man!

[Moving away from the school where he was 'The Man' allowed Billy to move on and establish himself with new peers who had no preconceived ideas of him.]

Increasing your teenager's commitment to school

Regardless of the study profile your teen fits, here are some universally applicable ways to increase teenagers' commitment to school.

Talk about your concerns

Although it's sometimes hard to resist the soapbox, encouragement works much better than lecturing.

Keep showing your support

I've seen thousands of students who have a 'bad' year return the next year remarkably refocused. Many parents have told me that, just when they were about to sell their teenager over the internet, they mysteriously returned from the dark place they'd been lost in. What makes the difference? It can be as simple as hearing about an appealing career, having a great holiday and recharging energy levels or having a positive talk with parents over the school break.

Help them establish short-term and long-term goals

Having goals gives teenagers something to aim for and look forward to. But make sure they are realistic and not pie-in-the-sky-stuff.

Show them what's around the corner

Often students have a greater choice of subjects and programs as they move up into the senior years at high school. I've seen the eyes of many students light up when they know choices will be more attractive a little further down the track. Suddenly it's worth hanging in there. Teenagers occasionally need help to focus on the bigger, more exciting picture.

Help them see the big picture

Teenagers often cheer up when they see what *school can do for them*. Investigate possible careers with them. If possible, visit sites with them where they can see the principles of what they are learning being put into practice—such as a dam, parliament, court, fisheries and wildlife centre. They may not know what they want to do or be, but show them that passing at school opens many doors down the track. One student returned from the summer holidays with such a different attitude to school that I couldn't resist asking his secret. 'James, I'm so pleased with your work. It's improving out of sight. You must have had a great holiday.' 'I did. My uncle's a builder. I worked on a house with him in the holidays and I decided I'm going to be an architect. I want to work at school this year.' (Better late than never . . . and he did work!)

Another student came to my office asking: 'I want a job like Jerry Maguire—the guy in that movie. How can I do that?' This student was a talented athlete who had never shown much interest in 'school stuff' as she called it. It made perfect sense that she was interested in a career related to the sports industry. It was amazing to see the transformation in her when we looked at the wide range of courses available in the sports industry. Be on the lookout for careers that might match the unique personality and talents of your teenager.

Help them keep up the study momentum

After starting high school, some students lose motivation when the initial novelty wears off, while others go through down periods in later years.

John Flanagan, principal

Most young people enjoy the first few months of high school but there is no doubt that, for some, a 'switch off' factor can kick in at some stage during the first year. Parents who have established a workable routine with their children will have the best chance of observing and monitoring a change in feelings about school. Routines established (hopefully through discussion and negotiation rather than being imposed autocratically) will have the greatest chance of success.

When and where to do homework, encouraging (without forcing) discussion about school, listening without coming in too quickly with a comment, watching out for big mood swings or signs of disenchantment—all these can help parents.

Help them increase the fun factor

When school becomes a drag, try encouraging teenagers to look around for opportunities that will make them feel good about themselves.

Mei-Lin Ooi, 21

What helped me be so motivated at high school? I guess my involvement in every activity I heard about sort of helped to make the average school day more interesting. Right from my first year at high school, every time a teacher announced a workshop or competition, I always paid attention and signed my name up. I did everything from being class captain to playing sport, cross-country running, being in the school band, building a racing car and taking a self-defence course. My parents were highly supportive and frequently getting my name in the school newsletter was good for conversations at mealtimes. At the time I didn't think all of this would have any impact on my life, but it has. When I was in my fourth year of high school I went for an interview for a part-time job with a multinational company. From my résumé and enthusiasm, they thought I was a university student rather than a little high-school kid. Getting involved in everything you can gives you confidence and shows you're a proactive person who loves a challenge. I've been paid to attend (worked at) four Grand Finals, four Formula 1 Grand Prix, and an Olympic Games! It's great fun, makes school less boring and does fabulous things to your ego! During those difficult years when peer pressure mounts, acne pops and voices break, I had a great time meeting new people, working and experiencing new things.

Don't compare your teenager's results with those of anyone else

This is particularly true of your own high-school results, their siblings, cousins or children of friends. This rarely works as an incentive to study harder. Praising teenagers for their own achievements is far more effective. They need to know it's not a competition.

Reality check

If results are borderline, find out what is required to enable students to progress to the next class. Students are sometimes shocked to find they cannot be promoted because of inadequate progress. Being informed *when there is still time to improve results* can motivate students to work harder.

Help them plan achievable steps to catch up and get back on track

Some teenagers believe they are so far behind that they give up. Students who are disorganised and don't know how to study effectively need help making plans and investigating ways to enhance their learning (see

Chapter 6). School counsellors can generally help with this, even acting as mentors. Show your teenager that you believe in them. The amount of work an energetic teenager can complete—*when they want to*—is amazing! It's almost never too late.

Show your interest

Be around and involved in their studies as much as possible. Teenagers often put on a 'get out of my face' façade when they still crave parental encouragement. The trick is to stand back just enough to allow them to feel more independent, but close enough to step in when needed.

Offer incentives

This may sound a tad like blackmail, but believe me it works. Think of it as 'positive reinforcement'. Take your teenager out for pizza *after* the major assignment is completed. But never let it sound like blackmail. 'Forget going out unless the work's done' won't have the same effect as 'Of course you can go out. We just want you to finish the work first.'

Give your teenager the opportunity to turn over a new leaf . . . as often as they need to

At the end of each semester or school year, help your teenager reassess their progress, set some new goals and make the *transition* more smoothly and confidently into the period ahead. If this is a positive discussion rather than a 'tell off' session, it may change their whole approach to school. I've seen many students return after the summer holidays with a noticeably fresh and enthusiastic approach. Most students want to do well at school. Sometimes they simply need some encouragement.

Encourage a get-up-and-go approach

Being physically active works magic for many teenagers. A 'solo' pursuit like surfing or swimming allows teenagers to work out pent up frustrations and lose themselves in a personal challenge. Team activities have the additional benefit of helping them make friends and feel more comfortable in social settings. All of this helps teenagers keep fit and have more energy to focus at school.

Jeffrey Emmel, national executive director, Australian Council for Health, Physical Education and Recreation

It is well known that teenagers who are regularly active generally feel good about themselves, are likely to concentrate better in class, learn a great deal about other teenagers and also learn to communicate well with others.

If your teenager appears to be losing focus or motivation for school, ask yourself:

Are my expectations clear and reasonable?

Not every teenager is an Einstein, and this shouldn't matter. There are far more important things in life—happiness for one! Teenagers should know they don't have an impossible academic mission to accomplish. If their self-esteem is crushed by the perception that they have let their parents down, or might let them down, the damage can be disastrous. I remember one student telling me that, when his school reports come out, two or three days can pass in his home when no one talks at mealtimes. 'The house goes really quiet.' He jokingly told me that he was getting used to this but the hurt in his voice was unmistakable. 'I'm not good at school Miss and that's why I muck around. My parents blame me for not trying but I'm no good at any of it.' (School is *not* that important!)

Teenagers who feel they can't deliver what is expected often give up. Tell your teenager you only want them to do their best. The key is to acknowledge the abilities of your teenager and to *help them to do the same*—all the while protecting their self-esteem.

Is the work becoming too difficult?

In my experience, it's sometimes difficult for parents to accept that their teenager may not have the ability to do better, or even want to continue their education. It's essential to be realistic about your teenager's abilities and help them choose subjects and courses they will enjoy and be able to experience a sense of success with.

Is this the best school for my teenager after all?

Ask them. Could another school offer programs they would enjoy more? Is their school delivering? (See the 'Is your teenager at the right school?' section later in this chapter.)

FAQs

Q: Friends tell us our son would do better in a single-sex high school where teaching styles cater for boys and have more hands-on activities. There are no boys-only schools in our area. Should we book him into a school that would involve extensive travelling on public transport or will he be okay at our local high school?

A: Co-ed schools are aware of the preferred learning styles of many boys and girls and generally ensure classes offer a good mix of teaching styles to engage all students. However, while students may have a preferred learning style, they must also be able to adjust to all teaching styles. Not all boys enjoy or flourish in a boys-only school, and there are many advantages in choosing the local school. Travelling long distances is very draining for growing teenagers and, in senior years, time becomes increasingly precious. More worrying is that your son would shift to high school without support from friends who will probably attend school locally. This could mean a lonely and unhappy time for him. Discuss everything with your son and allow him to make the final decision.

Professor Ron Rapee, Department of Psychology, Macquarie University

If a child is reporting difficulties with negative feelings about school, including feeling awkward or shy, worried, or sad and lonely, it is most important for parents not to trivialise or minimise these experiences. Parents should listen to their child openly and, if the feelings seem to be causing any difficulties for the child's life, they should talk to the school counsellor or a similar mental health expert. Good, specialised programs exist to help children and adolescents learn to cope with negative feelings and these programs can help many young people change their lives.

'Failing'

'Failing' is an awful term to use for a young person and should be banned! Good schools see the writing on the wall and let you know that your teenager is having *difficulty* with work while they still have time to catch up.

Some students are not academically inclined. I have a lot of sympathy for this group. They frequently come to see me for careers advice . . .

'Miss . . . I'm not very academic. What can I do?'

'What do you mean by that?'

'You know . . . I'm pretty dumb. I'm just no good at school, Miss.'

Sadly, many students interpret 'non-academic' as being *dumb*. Set the record straight. Not being good at formalised school learning with its various assessments, assignments and exams does *not* indicate that a student is dumb (see Chapter 2 on intelligence). Stories abound of teenagers who didn't do well at school and have gone on to become very successful in the 'real world'. They need to understand that not being 'school smart' is not the end of the world.

What can parents do when teenagers are floundering at school?

◎ Discuss everything with your teenager in a calm and supportive manner. Identify what's going on. Is this school catering to their interests and talents? Would they be happier and more successful at another school with different programs? Is something preventing them from concentrating on school?

◎ Ask your teenager how you can help them.

◎ Contact the school to discuss the situation. Welfare staff are generally a good starting point. Ensure your teenager feels comfortable about attending the meeting with you. This is not a 'tell off' session; it's a 'how can we help you' analysis. Good schools approach things this way.

◎ Devise an achievable plan of action with your teenager and the school. Can your teenager be given time to catch up or do extra work to achieve a pass? Can the situation be saved?

◎ Above all, do everything you can to protect your teenager's self-esteem. No one enjoys failing. Teenagers may appear not to care, but it's a well-rehearsed act. They do care and they do hurt.

◎ This is an opportunity to show your teenager you support them come what may. If the school is unsupportive or handles the situation insensitively, fight like hell to support your child. Students deserve to be treated with respect and given the opportunity to turn things around. This does not mean going into denial mode, though. It's essential that you and your teenager are honest about why they are in this position before they can move forward.

Q: My son excels at sport and is on top of the world playing basketball. Unfortunately his enthusiasm doesn't extend to school and his results are starting to fall. How can we stop this?

A: School results are relatively unimportant if your son is happy. I've met many parents who would give anything to see their teenager happy. But this shouldn't prevent you from discussing his future plans and encouraging him to put in enough work at school to ensure he passes and gets into courses and careers he would enjoy. Researching courses and careers in the sports industry would be a good starting point and may motivate him to give more attention to his studies. It would be a mistake to criticise his sporting involvement or make him drop these activities.

Is your teenager at the right school?

School should be about more than passing exams and obtaining scores. It should help teenagers develop and grow into confident and happy young adults. If you have done everything you can to help your teenager be more motivated and happier at their school, and they are still not gaining as much as you would hope from the experience, it may be time to consider other schools.

Numerous studies show the importance of a caring school

- When teenagers feel valued and cared about at school this increases their resilience and protects them from high risk-taking.[6]
- Students who believe they are not cared about at school are *four times* more likely to suffer depressive symptoms.[7]
- Teenagers who feel supported by teachers and other support staff at school are more motivated to succeed academically.[8]

Evaluate your teenager's school

It's enlightening to take a step back occasionally and evaluate what is going on in your teenager's world at school. If there is something compromising the interests of your teenager, it may be time to move them to another school where they will feel more 'at home'. Making this decision can take months of talking, meetings with school counsellors at the current school and investigation of other possible schools.

If you have a gut feeling that your child isn't happy, do everything you can to work out what is going on and how you can help them be happier about school. The next time you ask your teenager, 'How's school?' pay particular attention to their response.

Some questions to ask in deciding if your teenager is at the best school

- Are they really enjoying school or simply killing time?
- Do they feel cared about at their school?
- Are they being bullied?
- Does the school allow them to thrive rather than simply survive?
- Are they feeling under-challenged or out of their depth?
- Is the school complementary to their passions, aspirations and abilities?
- Are they caught up with a peer group that is 'a bad influence'?
- Do they have an intensely competitive sibling at the school?
- Do they feel at ease with the aspirations and outlooks of the students at the school or are they a fish out of water?

Schools vary incredibly. Teenagers also come in very different packages. Some thrive in very academic schools while they would be bored and perhaps even argumentative in a less academic setting. A mother recently told me that her daughter's first year at high school was a nightmare:

Anna isn't into pop culture and teen girl gossip. She's a thinker and loves reading and acquiring new knowledge. She just isn't like most of the girls at her school and says she doesn't feel part of the school. Kids do a lot of group work these days and the girls say, 'Don't go with Anna. She'll make you work too much!' Anna came to us and after a lot of soul searching and discussion we've just arranged for her to start at a new school next year. She's looking forward to it already.

Another parent told me her son had left a school where peers openly referred to him as 'the smart arse' because he loved learning. In some schools, the tall poppy syndrome is alive and well while in others academic achievement and learning are valued. Conversely, some teenagers flounder in academic schools when they would be on top of the world at a school that offered more hands-on programs.

Sometimes it's the overall 'flavour' of a school that can alienate some teenagers. Some respond well to conservative schools and will happily wear colour-coordinated socks and look immaculate each day. Other teenagers detest discipline and will fight school rules all the way, sometimes spending more time in detention over the jewellery, dyed hair and wrong-coloured socks than they do studying.

Does the curriculum cater for your teenager?

While the flavour of a school is an extremely important consideration for young people, having subjects or programs that make them want to come to school can prevent many headaches. No two schools are alike. There may be a school in your area that could help your teenager find their niche area of interest and have their first positive experience of schooling. I have also known many students who have decided that it was worth travelling several hours each day to attend a school where they found programs they loved. Here are a few suggestions to consider:

Vocational courses

Many schools now have very practical vocational education and training courses to suit all interests: Automotive, Building and Construction, Engineering, Equine Industry, Multimedia, Information Technology, Hospitality, Business Office Administration, Fitness, Community Services, Concept Development for Clothing Products and many others. Because of their practical nature, vocational courses can make learning seem more *relevant* to young people. They are nationally recognised and results contribute to students' overall scores if they decide to go on and complete the final year of high school. Students continue to study a range of subjects at school as well as vocational courses. Sometimes students leave school for a day or afternoon each week to attend classes at local institutes offering trade and technical courses.

Many students re-engage with learning after attending their first vocational training sessions while previously they were at risk of dropping out of school. Vocational courses have been shown to be an excellent option for all students, from those struggling at school to those above average academically, increasing students' self-confidence and positive view of learning.[9]

Special programs

There are some excellent programs for students who don't enjoy mainstream high school. These are often in very supportive environments where students are provided with individual counselling and self-paced programs. Contact your regional Department of Education and inquire about programs available.

Anne Broadribb, manager, The Island Work Education and Training Unit

In our program, students who have dropped out of mainstream schools or who are at risk of dropping out rediscover a passion for learning. When they learn new skills and have that feeling of success . . . they begin to gain a sense of worth and achievement. Their lives literally start to turn around.

Ensure your teenager isn't unhappy at school or doesn't want to leave school early because they are in a school that doesn't suit their personality, interests or abilities. Clearly it's important for teenagers to feel accepted by peers, and this is generally more likely to happen when they have similar expectations of school and similar aspirations and interests.

'M.L.S.', 21

I was never into the whole academic scene at school. I couldn't sit at a desk and study for hours on end. It just wasn't me. I preferred to be creative and perform. At the academic school I attended this was not at all appreciated; rather, it was looked down upon. I threw myself into the limited creative programs they provided only to be accepted into one then rejected for the next. I decided I was going to show them that I was better. I saw an advertisement for a well-known music group and program out of school. I was adamant that I wanted to audition. I attended the daunting audition held by a strict woman and was accepted and finally praised for my talents.

As time went by I noticed I also had a flair for art and drama. The art studio for me was a safe haven. It was the only place where I could turn up the music and paint, draw and sculpt without feeling the stress around me. I didn't enjoy school. If I had my chance again I would find a school that accepts students for who they are, cherishes their talents and makes them feel good about themselves.

How should parents approach choosing a new school?

The most important consideration is to protect the self-esteem of your teenager. They should *never* be made to feel that something is wrong with them or that they don't fit in. The trick is to turn the situation around and make it a *positive* experience. Their current school simply isn't the right school for them. Handled well, this can be a real turning point in your teenager's life.

I have come across many reasons why parents have considered another school for their teenagers. In every case, the most successful outcome occurs when teenagers are involved in all discussions and are allowed to make the final choice. Forcing a teenager to stay at or leave a particular school is rarely successful. Teenagers are more likely to commit themselves to study or other areas of their lives when they are able to have a say in what happens to them. It's important to:

- involve them in all discussions and investigation of alternative schools;
- support them at all times;

- reassure them that together you will find a better school;
- allow them to make the final call;
- encourage them to see the new school as *a new beginning*.

Sandra, parent

Just before the end of the year Helen came to us and said she didn't want to go back to her school the next year. This came out of the blue because she seemed to have made plenty of friends, had joined the school band and was going well academically. In reality, Helen did not socialise with school friends outside of school hours. This was mainly because we lived in between the 'city' and the 'country'. Students from Helen's school tended to come from rural areas and rode their horses all weekend. Helen still had more social interaction with friends from primary school days who had, in the main, gone to the bigger 'city' school—still accessible by car.

We decided that if Helen was going to change schools, she should go to the school that had the largest group of her friends. I rang mothers of students there and we spoke at length. All students were very happy and would welcome Helen joining them. She was booked into the new school and we went shopping for new uniforms and books . . .

As the school year loomed, I think I was more nervous than Helen. It was a scary time. I vividly remember dropping Helen off at the gate on the first day and watching her walk in alone. I drove home with tears in my eyes hoping that we had made the right decision and she would be happy. I needn't have worried. She settled in quickly, her friends making the transition easy, and she hasn't looked back.

Helen, 15 (Sandra's daughter)

Now don't get me wrong . . . the first school was great but it just didn't suit me. I had friends but they had different interests to mine. They liked horses. I like art. I guess that's the main reason I wanted to change schools. I wasn't unhappy but I wasn't happy enough. And if you're not happy then you won't strive to your full potential. Moving schools was the best thing I could have done.

Kier Houghton, 21

When I was accepted into the high school of my dreams, I thought my life was set. But repeatedly we were told that each year was counting down to the dreaded final year at school. This would mean less socialising and hour upon hour of study. I wasn't sure that this was what I wanted even though I was generally a motivated student with excellent grades.

Looking back on that time in my life, I was not very happy. Family and friends started noticing that I wasn't my usual self. Oddly enough, as I sit here trying to recall details of the first three years at high school, I can't. They're not there . . .

During the summer break I met some new friends who went to a different kind of school. As they told me of their experiences I liked what I heard and wanted to know more. I got online and checked out the school's website. It was very unlike my school. There wasn't such a focus on getting the highest scores or on how many science rooms there were on campus. The site seemed to be an endless display of creativity. It listed subjects I never knew existed. I was definitely interested.

I had to break the news to the parents. I remember them being a little worried as to why I wanted to change schools. I told them I wasn't happy at my school. I could see that they weren't fully convinced so I broke out the big guns. Being a resourceful teenager, I explained that my school didn't offer the subjects I wanted to do and this would severely dampen any chance of getting into the course I wanted. (This wasn't too far off the truth.) They agreed to go and have a look around the new school.

We went on tours of the new school. It wasn't nearly as shiny as my school but inside the old rundown buildings was a completely different story. I saw kids not in school uniform, free to express themselves. I heard teachers being called by their first names. I saw students talking to teachers with honest respect and teachers talking to students as equals. But most importantly I saw students with smiles on their faces. I made my decision.

On that last day I walked out of my old school, the biggest weight was suddenly lifted off my shoulders. As the summer break drew to an end I didn't have the usual increasing dread of the upcoming year—I was kind of excited. I felt like I had taken control of my life.

I had a great time at my new school. The last years flew by and they were my best years of schooling. I obtained a result that allowed me to get into the tertiary course I wanted and at the end of last year I graduated. Within a week of graduation I was offered employment. As I move now into this next phase of my life I can't help but be thankful for the kid I was back at my first high school. I'm almost certain that if I hadn't had the balls to make a decision to change schools—and if I hadn't had the support from my family and friends during that period—I wouldn't be where I am today—happy.

FAQs

Q: Our son is a high achiever. Should we take him out of his current school and send him to one with a special program for gifted students?
A: Only if your son is bored and wants to go to another school should you consider moving him. There is evidence that some gifted students don't develop to their full potential if they are not sufficiently challenged.[10] But if he is happy at his current school and surrounded by friends, it could be counterproductive to take him out of this environment. Even gifted students need friends far more than any special program. Ask your son how he feels. Another possibility is to investigate university extension programs he may be able to complete while remaining at his current school. Win-win situations are always nice if you can find them.

Q: Our daughter wants to move to another school. How do we know this is not just a 'bad patch' she'll get over? We don't want to move her unnecessarily.
A: Discuss the reasons why she wants to move schools and reassure her that you want the best outcome for her. Make it clear that you believe this is a big decision and you want her and yourself to have time to think things through carefully so that the right decision is made. Sometimes taking time to discuss issues and investigate other schools allows teenagers time to realise that what has been worrying them can be sorted out and they decide to remain at their current school. Teenagers

crave reassurance and attention, especially from parents. Even making an appointment with your daughter's school counsellor or careers counsellor may be enough to make her see that many people do care about her. Often nothing makes a teenager feel better about being at their school and gives them a greater confidence boost than a little TLC.

Wanting to leave school early

Most parents assume their children will complete high school. They are terrified by the prospect of teenagers wanting to leave early. And there are distinct advantages to completing high school education. A recent Australian report, *How Young People are Faring 2004*, found that young people who do not complete high school education are twice as likely to be unemployed.[11] Yet, for some teenagers who feel school has nothing more to offer them, leaving seems the more logical path. Forcing teenagers to stay at school when their heart isn't in it can be counterproductive. Leaving with dignity, their self-esteem intact and an identified pathway to follow are the keys to preventing much angst—and unemployment—for young people in the future.

If your teenager seems adamant about leaving school early, listen calmly and without making any judgments. It could be a fleeting fancy, but it could also be a desperate plea for your consent and support.

When teenagers are adamant about wanting to leave school early, and all alternative schools and programs have been investigated, parents must *support them*. It can be a tough and lonely time and often they won't realise this until it hits them (see Chapter 12 for more discussion about the transition to work). Students leaving before the completion of high school miss the celebrations of peers leaving school together. Leaving school is a significant time for everyone, a rite of passage that should be 'celebrated' and marked in some special way. Parents may not feel like celebrating, but what happens during this period can have lasting effects on a young person. The situation must be viewed *positively*. This is the best way to maximise a young person's likelihood of one day returning to some form of further education and training.

A quiet revolution is occurring in some countries as increasing numbers of students who have had negative experiences at school are finding courses that suit them at vocational training institutes. Courses can help teenagers regain a positive image of learning and be the start of a pathway that can lead on to further study and exciting employment options at various exit points along the way. Many courses allow students to work at their own pace in classes where the learning environment is more adult-oriented. This is very appealing to students who dislike the whole notion of rules about uniform, attendance checks and the other formalities most schools adhere to. When we consider the whole notion of lifelong learning as being a fundamental requirement for our fast-moving and constantly changing world, any course that might re-instil an enjoyment of learning is certainly worth investigating.

In Australia, these vocational training institutes are known as TAFE (Technical and Further Education) institutes. In Britain they are known as polytechnics. The status of Australian TAFE institutes is increasing, as some courses are being accredited as degrees. Students can begin their studies in vocational certificate or diploma courses and then complete degrees in their interest area at the TAFE institute. Many students also elect to transfer to universities and are given credit for their TAFE studies, reducing the length of study needed to graduate with a degree. This is encouraging news for students who don't qualify to enter university courses directly after high school.

The news in Britain is even more exciting. In 1992, a British Higher Education Act signalled the end of the perceived gulf between universities and polytechnics. Since then, over 30 polytechnics have achieved university status, many outperforming established universities in league tables.

Parents clearly need to encourage teenagers to consider courses at all institutes in the search for a course that suits the unique needs and talents of their teenagers. To ignore a course simply because it is at a particular institution could diminish a teenager's chances of finding the course and career of their dreams.

A five-step plan for teenagers who want out of school

1. Be willing to consider alternatives

Suggest that your teenager remain at school for a mutually agreed time so that options can be investigated. Agree to reassess things at the end of term or end of the year. Most students will agree to stay for a set time once they know their parents are willing to seriously discuss the leaving school proposal. This gives parents time to discover why teenagers are unhappy and identify the best solutions. It can also release pent-up pressure that has led to the decision to leave in the first place, allowing teenagers to see things more clearly.

2. Identify the reason for wanting to leave school

Don't assume anything. Your teenager may be good at hiding real problems in their life, both in and out of school. Sometimes talking through issues can release some of the stress they are feeling and they may decide to stay at school. Not all teenagers want to leave school because of academic capabilities. Some leave because they lack a connection with teachers and peers. The most powerful incentive for students to remain at school despite not being in love with the place is the social aspect—being with their friends.[12] Surveys of teenagers who have left school early are very telling. When asked if there is one thing that would have kept them at school, many also cite more caring teachers.[13] Once again, ask yourself whether your teenager is in a school where they feel cared about by teachers and where they are with like-minded peers rather than those who have very different aspirations, backgrounds or abilities.

3. Speak to counsellors or welfare staff

Ideally, do this with your consenting teenager. As they so frequently tell me, *'It's my life! I should have a say!'* Sometimes, in their desire to feel independent and grown-up, they may prefer to speak to counsellors privately. What's important is that they know you care.

4. Speak to the careers counsellor

Good careers advice is invaluable for teenagers. I've seen teenagers leave my office with renewed determination to do well at school when they have *some idea* of what they want to do. They don't have to identify a particular career. Even knowing about the wonderful opportunities available can enthuse young people. Help your teenager investigate various pathways and levels of education needed to enter careers. This turns the question around to: 'What can school do for you?' For some students this makes all the difference in the world.

A student came to see me determined to leave school immediately. Her mother looked traumatised. Simone wanted to be a beauty therapist and had heard it was easy to get into. She was shocked to hear she must complete high school to study beauty therapy. 'Oh well, I guess I better start studying then.' (Mum could barely contain her joy.) It was interesting that Simone was supremely confident that she could pass *if she wanted to* ... and she did!

5. *Put your teenager in charge (with fingers crossed)*

Teenagers respond a thousand times more positively *if they believe the final decision will be theirs.* Many elect to stay at school because the process of investigating 'to leave or not to leave' highlights the advantages of staying and brings them closer to their parents. Being allowed to think about leaving can be a valuable process. If handled sensitively, it can reinforce a teenager's desire to hang in there.

FAQ: Our daughter has completely lost interest in school and wants to leave. She only has a year to go before completing secondary school. Should we make her stay at school?

A: Red alert! Making a teenager do anything is usually a fruitless exercise regardless of how sensible and valuable it would be for them. Teenagers *detest* being forced into anything unless it's a pair of very tight, very 'in' jeans. Work through the five-step plan. But if your daughter is still determined to leave, it's generally best to allow her this choice. Tell her that you will always support her if she changes her mind, but also show interest and help her through the process of obtaining employment. It's not an easy process and may even convince her to remain at school after all. She may also go into the workforce and end up running the company where she works, or she may decide to go back to study in a year or two. Whatever happens, don't allow your relationship to become a casualty of this situation.

Elizabeth Grant, parent

I have never cried more than when Daniel said he wanted to leave school. He wasn't studying, he was always in trouble and I was constantly being called up to the school. He would do anything to get out of homework, even the housework. I've never seen anyone clean a house like Daniel. I considered sending him to another school but he said, 'Mum, I just don't want to'. A year on, I can't believe how happy he is. I haven't seen him this happy—ever. In his pre-apprenticeship course at TAFE he got marks like 98 in every subject. He started a three-month probation period with a motor mechanic but after three days the boss wanted to sign the apprenticeship papers. He wouldn't study at school but now he shows such a lot of pride in his work. The boss has given him the keys to the workshop. He was so proud. He's a different person and we're thrilled.

The good news is that I've met numerous parents like Elizabeth who can't wait to tell me how wonderful it is to see their teenagers happy and enjoying what they are doing. They often use the word 'miracle' in describing the transformation. Sometimes school simply isn't the right place for a young person at this particular time in their lives. *Allowing them to leave gives them a chance to find their niche in the world or perhaps even discover that they want to return to study after all.* And it's an entirely different prospect when they *choose* to study rather than being forced. Freedom of choice unlocks great energy and determination in young people.

Daniel Grant, 18 (Elizabeth's son)

I've always loved cars and working with my hands. When I started at the workshop, I thought 'This is what I want to be doing'. It's a million times better than school. It's perfect.

FAQ: My son says he hates school and wants to leave and get a job. How can I convince him that not completing high school will severely limit his future options?

A: I frequently meet ex-students who have returned to study after working for a number of years. These students share an intense desire to study and a level of commitment almost impossible to find in younger teenagers. A great message to give your teenager is that it's *never* too late to go back to study. Leaving school early doesn't necessarily signal the end of their formal education *provided their self-esteem is protected through* *this process.* Do lots of talking and find out exactly why your teenager hates school. Ultimately, if he is determined to leave, make sure you support him through the entire process.

Dr Damon Cartledge, La Trobe University

I scan my new university business cards—'Dr Damon Cartledge—Senior Lecturer'—and wonder if anyone will know the satisfaction that gives me.

In 1993 I was a technical school dropout with a good job but no marketable qualifications. I remember sitting in the carpark before my first university lecture full of self-doubt and apprehension. But I also remember the feeling of inspired self-worth after that first class: I could do this. By the end of 2002 I had accumulated one certificate, two Advanced Certificates, two Diplomas, a Bachelor's degree, a Master's degree and a Doctorate. What if I had finished the final year at school at age 17? I don't know the answer, other than to suggest that I don't feel I would have been ready for the intellectual rigor of university. It took my family and I ten years' hard work but it was a journey rich with learning and experiences of life.

After leaving school early, Damon worked as a pastrycook and then as a musician in the army before considering further study. The rest is history. Damon's story is not uncommon. Some students are simply not ready for higher education at 17 or 18; yet, at some point down the track, they may return with a real enthusiasm for further study.

If your teenager's self-esteem isn't damaged by the experience of leaving school early, there's always a chance they will return to study down the track when they are ready.

Patty Gray, parent

At the start of Jack's second last year at high school, I could no longer get him to go to school. Even if I could coax him out of bed, he would spend the day elsewhere. By this stage he was becoming ill over the whole school thing. He was unable to sleep and seemed depressed.

Eventually my husband and I spoke with Jack and acknowledged his position of refusing to go to school. He wanted to officially leave school and go to work. This terrified us. What sort of job would he be able to get? Would he be locked in unskilled positions for the rest of his life? Like a gift from heaven, the boss at Jack's Saturday job offered him an apprenticeship.

Jack no longer complains of being unable to sleep. While any attempt at a chat concerning school would result in a string of expletives and stalking off, Jack now freely chats when he gets home from work explaining everything in great detail and spontaneously showing us items he has made. People comment on how well he looks and how his confidence has developed. As part of Jack's journey to manhood, the apprenticeship is a positive force and proof for himself and others of his ability to apply himself, work hard and be independent and creative in the real marketplace.

Gareth Bowen, 18

I left school at the beginning of my final year of high school. Family reasons . . . I started working full-time in the hospitality industry and learnt a lot about time management and discipline. I had time to think and it made me a much more relaxed but determined person. Before leaving school, I had lots of stress and no real focus. After a year out of school, I'm now at the point where I want to go back and complete my last year.

[Gareth returned to high school and completed his final year at school very successfully, receiving several awards for outstanding achievement in music.]

In essence

All teenagers are unique and come into their own study stride at different times. The right support from parents at difficult times can help teenagers turn things around, find their feet and be off and running again.

Failure is success if we learn from it.
—Malcolm S. Forbes

Part V

THE SENIOR YEARS
supporting teenagers at school and beyond

10

Future directions—subjects, courses, careers

Education is what remains after one has forgotten everything he learned in school.

—Albert Einstein

There is a huge over-emphasis on school results in the final years at school by everyone—schools, teachers, parents, the public and the media. It's so easy to allow the results hysteria to overshadow what should be the central purpose of school: *to educate* young people. The Oxford definition of 'educate' is 'to give intellectual and moral training to'. Out of curiosity, I frequently ask friends to identify the most valuable things they gained from their high-school education. I also ask ex-students the same question when I meet them a year or more after having completed their *education*. Not one has ever mentioned results in their answers! Most have realised how unimportant those once all-important results actually are.

If not results, what do people mention as being the most valuable things they gained from high school? Some say a particular teacher taught them how to weigh up all sides of an issue before making an ethical decision, others describe a teacher who taught them to stand up for their beliefs while respecting the beliefs of others. Many mention teachers who were so passionate about their subject areas that they also learnt to value the discovery of new knowledge. I remember one ex-student telling me that the most important thing she learnt from her English teacher was to be proud of being an individual and also to value hard work. These are the things that make up a real education and we must bring the focus back to them if we are to equip young people to be intellectual and moral members of society. Teenagers need to know that scores are not as important as being socially, politically and morally responsible young adults. These are the things that can set a young person up for life, not a single score obtained in one particular year.

What is important through all of this is that teenagers are encouraged to be true to themselves and to be confident enough to take opportunities that come along as they make their way in the world beyond the school gates. The role of parents and schools is to support teenagers and to encourage them to take those steps, make those decisions and above all to be happy and enjoy the ride. Let's look at strategies parents can use to support teenagers as they make decisions about the two main areas of concern in the final years at school:

- selecting subjects;
- identifying courses and careers.

Helping teenagers select subjects and identify courses and careers

Teenagers today have thousands of courses from which to select. New career areas are being created each year. All of this can be simultaneously exciting and overwhelming for teenagers. The trick is knowing about *choices* and *pathways*. Students who understand the flexibility of pathways beyond high school are less stressed and can enjoy investigating various possibilities. There is an enormous amount of information to absorb, and parents can be an invaluable support through this process.

FAQ: How can teenagers select the right subjects when they still don't know what they want to do?
A: Fortunately, many tertiary courses don't have any prerequisites apart from English. If your teenager selects subjects they enjoy and are good at, they maximise their chances of doing well and therefore being able to gain entry to a wider selection of courses. I've seen many students become highly stressed because they chose subjects someone told them were 'good' subjects and dropped those they enjoyed.

Teenagers should progressively investigate various career opportunities, and hopefully these investigations will uncover their career interest before completing high school. If they still feel unsure about which career to pursue at the end of high school, they can select generalist courses such as Arts, Commerce or Science that lead on to many different careers. Taking some time out to work and travel may also provide an opportunity to discover the career of their dreams. Sometimes students discover this career in the most unlikely place.

Reassure your teenager that it is common for students *not* to know what career they want to pursue. It is not always possible or even desirable for a teenager of 16 or 17 to know what they might or might not enjoy career-wise. Unfortunately, 'What do you want to be?' is a question fired at young people right from the time they can barely talk! I counsel many highly stressed students who worry they might 'get it wrong'. The good news is that educational pathways are more flexible these days. It's possible to enter a particular course and then transfer to a new course if they discover one that appeals to them more. There are also exciting postgraduate courses for people to pursue and change career direction. Students are so much happier and more relaxed when they see that they won't be locked forever in the first course or career they enter.

Mark Giantsis, 27

After finishing high school, I tried many jobs—joinery, shop fitting, steelwork, labouring. Basically I was feeling my way around. Then my great-grandmother became ill. She was dying and after work I'd pop over to the nursing home to be with her and look after her. I started thinking that nursing might not be too bad and spoke to dad about it. He gave me the encouragement I needed and everything fell into place after that. I went back to study and here I am. My family have always been supportive and said, 'Wherever you're happy . . . go for it!' I enjoy nursing for now but might even move on to something else in the future—another specialisation in nursing or something really different. Who knows . . .

FAQs

Q: How can I help my son to select the right subjects at school?

A: The golden rule is: *Students should select subjects they are interested in and enjoy.* It's difficult for teenagers to study subjects they dislike or find difficult. Students should investigate the content of subjects by talking to other students and teachers. It's important to follow their heart, but also to make an informed choice.

Q: What happens if your teenager is not good at a subject required by a particular tertiary course?

A: If they simply require a pass in this subject rather than a high score, they may be able to manage it. However, if this subject is going to require so much time input that other subjects suffer, they may be disadvantaged and miss out on selection into courses entirely. Tertiary institutions sometimes require different prerequisites. Help your teenager identify similar courses that do *not* require this subject. It's also important to think about *why* the subject is a prerequisite in the first place. If it is because the course itself requires a high level of ability in this area, your teenager may struggle in the course.

Q: Our daughter has no idea what she wants to be. How can we help?

A: Teenagers all mature at different times. They *don't* have to know what they want to be at 15, 19 or even 20. Many students transfer from one course into another, changing their minds many times before finding their first dream course and career. In today's world, few people will remain in the same career or job for life and there is increasing recognition of our need to become lifelong learners. Once again, what young people will need to be successful in the world of work are transferable skills and a willingness to adapt and change as required in each job.

Some teenagers have a strong sense of where they want to go after school and what their aspirations are. Others are happy to drift for a year or so until they find their feet and identify a clear direction. The best way for you to help your daughter is to help her become well-informed by progressively investigating careers. Encourage her to see this process as a challenge rather than an obstacle and to keep in mind the activities and situations she enjoys. Is she outgoing, reserved, inquisitive or sociable (see Chapters 1 and 5)? Sometimes this will give her insights into careers she may enjoy. Students who are very social and interested in sport may love a career in sports management, physiotherapy or even sports journalism. Those interested in people and social issues may enjoy social work, psychology, nursing or even environmental engineering.

Encourage your teenager to speak to people working in various careers. Neighbours, relatives or lecturers in tertiary courses are all good people to approach for information. Encourage her to ask questions:

◎ What do you most enjoy about your work?
◎ What are the difficult aspects of your work?
◎ What is a typical day like in this career?
◎ Where can I find employment in this career area?
◎ Is it possible to specialise in different areas in this career?
◎ Are there any proposed changes to courses leading into this career?
◎ What are the most important skills or qualities required in this career?
◎ Could I visit your workplace or spend a day or two observing your work in action?
◎ Where can I get more information on courses leading into this career?
◎ Are you happy you chose this field to work in?

Q: Our son has always wanted to be a doctor but is worried about the high scores needed for medical courses. How can we help him?
A: Apart from giving him the best chances to maximise his entrance scores, you can help him identify *pathways* that lead into medicine. There are pathways and courses that lead into every career and finding these offers students great reassurance. Does he also know that there are postgraduate courses leading into medicine? Knowing that careers can be entered down the track reassures students that everything isn't riding on results obtained in one year. All students need a Plan B and C and D . . . and then some more!

Also bear in mind that students who say they have *always* wanted to enter a particular career are sometimes disappointed when they enter the course, especially if they haven't asked those important questions about the career and the day-to-day work involved.

A number of ex-students have told me that they regret entering a particular career (usually dictated by their entrance score) without having first investigated other career possibilities.

Q: My son keeps hearing that employment is falling in some career areas. How can we help him cope with all of this and choose wisely?

A: Employment prospects are an increasing concern for teenagers. Students often ask questions like: 'Miss, do you think there'll be jobs in this career? Is this a risky area to get into?' Some students allow their decisions about courses and careers to be limited by ideas about employment opportunities, which may not even apply when they will complete their course. Industries will also be created that don't even exist today and it is already an accepted fact that today's teenagers will not be in particular jobs or careers for life. Encourage your son to look at the *positive* aspects of all of this. A sound education will give him skills that will allow him to adapt to employment changes and enjoy newly emerging opportunities in the marketplace.

Q: Our daughter wants to go into a career where we believe she will be wasting her talents. How can we show her the advantages of better choices?

A: Allow your teenager to choose a career direction free of pressure. The movie *Billy Elliot* is a powerful reminder of the importance of allowing a young person to follow their heart.

Demand in career areas can also change. You might not be able to think of anything worse than her chosen career, but better a happy chef in the family than a grumpy engineer. And teenagers often change their mind two, three or more times before finally settling on a career—their *first* career, that is.

Recently an ex-student returned to see me. He had almost completed a double degree at a prestigious university. I immediately remembered him as being an outstandingly talented art student. After four and a half unhappy years in the course *his parents had chosen for him*, he finally found the courage to tell them his feelings. He *hated* his course and had decided to leave home, find a job and support himself while returning to study art. His parents were shocked. They were genuinely unaware of their son's unhappiness and his desperate desire to study art. A lack of communication had created a gulf between them and the son they loved. Of course they wanted him to be happy! Of course they didn't want him to leave home! There was a good ending to this story but I continue to see students trying to live lives and follow paths to please their parents. In these situations, everyone loses.

Samuel Krum, 23

Going into tertiary study, the overwhelming feeling for me was uncertainty. I was 18 and felt I was being made to choose my life's path *right then* and God help me if I made the wrong decision. Luckily I have parents who told me I would change my mind dozens of times and I should concentrate on having as much fun as possible during the years following high school. They told me the right path would present itself. I changed from Media to Music Industry to Music Performance and only now, at 23, do I feel like I know what I want to do.

Q: Our daughter is already worried about her final results at high school and she has three years to go before graduating. How can we help her?

A: Your task is a hefty one. You need to address the *score scam*. Students start comparing entry scores at various tertiary institutions and trying to predict how much each course will go up years before they reach the final year at school. Convince your daughter that there is life even after a lowish score.

Does she believe that everything doesn't hinge on a single score? Unfortunately many students are scared their life will 'disappear down the toilet' if they don't obtain high scores in the final year of school. They want proof that this isn't the case. Here is some information that should offer your daughter reassurance.

Some encouraging research is being conducted at Monash University by Stuart Levy and Julie Murray. In 1999, the Diploma of Foundation Studies, a one-year full-time course, was established for students whose results were not high enough to allow them entry directly into university. The course aimed to support students during the critical transition period to university and equip them with skills needed to succeed—skills such as essay writing, exam preparation, problem-solving, critical thinking and effective communication. How did these students fare? Remarkably well. This program indicates that a low score at the completion of high school does *not* necessarily indicate that a student is incapable of succeeding at university. The retention rates and academic performance of these students were comparable with students who obtained significantly higher scores at the completion of high school. Students classified as 'low achievers' at high school were as successful as those classified as 'high achievers'. This is great news for students. A low score isn't the end of the world, and certainly isn't always an accurate indication of ability to succeed at the tertiary level.[1]

Dr Stuart Levy, lecturer, Diploma of Foundation Studies, School of Humanities, Communication and Social Sciences, Monash University

Every year I am confronted with a number of students whose self-esteem and confidence have been ravaged by the vagaries of the tertiary admission ranking system. Many of these students go on to perform quite well in their university studies because motivation and a desire to succeed, rather than the score with which they gained entry, is the defining characteristic of a successful student. Indeed, for some students, low scores provide the motivation to transform them into a successful student precisely *because* they feel that they have something to prove.

Helping teenagers approach senior years with confidence

The ability to do well academically doesn't automatically guarantee a teenager's success out of school. These years present the perfect opportunity to encourage your teen to broaden their horizons and develop a future-oriented mindset in preparation for university and work life.

I have seen many students graduate from high school with flying colours only to flounder at the tertiary level or in the workforce. They were unable to think independently, to make decisions and to face challenges and uncertainty with a resilient and optimistic attitude. During the last two or three years at high school, parents can help teenagers develop attitudes and skills that will stand by them not only in the challenging years right after high school, but throughout their lives.

Helping teenagers manage stress

The negative effects of prolonged periods of stress have been shown to impede learning and weaken the immune system. Excessive worry and stress inhibit academic performance.[2]

It's important to notice when your teenager's stress levels are on the rise and talk to them about stress management. Some students unwind through sport, listening to music, self-talk, yoga, tai chi or climbing a tree. Others need to be reminded to take time out occasionally or to have a study-free weekend.

Many students tell me that they are embarrassed to admit to friends and parents that they are feeling stressed. 'All of my friends are fine. I'm the only one not coping.' It's a good idea for parents to occasionally ask teenagers how they are faring with the demands of study and exams. Letting them know that it's normal for everyone to sometimes feel worried can encourage them to share their feelings.

And whatever happened to having some fun along the way? I recently asked a class of senior students what they did for fun and was shocked by the baffled looks on many faces: 'Oh we don't have time for that Miss.' There is something terribly wrong when students believe that time away from study is a waste of time. And if the price of obtaining high scores is eliminating the fun times that should accompany youth, the price is way too high. Helping your teenager find ways to unwind gives them an advantage over other students because they will be in a better position to handle the demands of senior study. Tell them that everyone can learn how to relax. It simply takes a little investigation to identify what works best for each person.

Helping teenagers be positive about the future

Does your teenager really believe there are endless possibilities in life? Extensive research highlights the sad fact that some young people today have lost the ability to even imagine a positive future, resulting in growing levels of hopelessness, depression and ultimately suicide.[3] There is also clear evidence that actively encouraging young people to focus on the positives can enable them to internalise positive images and reduce feelings of hopelessness.[4] Encourage your teenager to focus on the excitement the future contains rather than the obstacles. Students who have goals and dreams are streets ahead of those who have a narrow, pessimistic view.

Helping teenagers identify specific goals and work towards them

If your teenager hasn't any goals by this stage, now is certainly the time to help them along. These may be career goals, planning for a GAP year, landing a better job or even improving their fitness. It's not the goal itself that is important but the experience of working hard for something and the feeling of satisfaction this brings. Teenagers develop determination when they learn to work and fight for something they want.

Jacinta Cross, 15

Writing has always been a means of expression, reflection and communication for me. In many ways it's been my anchor. Before I allow myself to be discouraged, I remember various times when people have told me they've connected with my writing—that gives me a feeling of purpose and confidence in myself. I am capable of something. Because writing is a relatively difficult field to get into, it's motivated me to learn as much as possible, take advantage of every opportunity and produce the best work I possibly can. This extends to other subjects at school. Recognition as an author is certainly something to aim for.

Helping teenagers develop moral intelligence and find meaning

Teenagers during this period start to search for meaning in their lives and a basis for making decisions about how to live good and moral lives. Surprisingly, many even search for answers on the internet.[5] Teenagers who are accustomed to discussing moral and ethical questions at home generally have a firmer personal belief system and are able to make more informed choices about all areas of their life, school included. Importantly, they are also less likely to succumb to peer pressure. Having a clear set of values enables students to be more confident and to develop an inner strength they can draw on during these challenging years.

In my work as a teacher and careers counsellor, students who come from families where issues are discussed openly and in a non-judgmental manner stand out from the crowd. These are the young people who have opinions but are also prepared to listen to differing viewpoints. Allow your teenagers to express their opinions at home knowing you will listen and help them clarify, modify or even alter views in a supportive environment.

Schools should also play an integral part in challenging teenagers to refine and develop their own belief system. Recently there has been much discussion internationally about values education in schools. One recent report again highlights the importance of schools and parents in providing young people with values education. Significantly, research indicates that parental influence over teenagers in values formation far outweighs that of schools.[6] Parents should know what is being taught in their teenagers' school. Education is about more than scores, passing exams and getting into jobs or courses. A good education also gives young people a set of ethics that will make them stand out as people of conviction.

FAQs

Q: What can parents do when they cannot approve of particular opinions, wishes or behaviour of their teenagers?

A: This can be an agonising position for a parent and there is no easy answer. It's crucial to provide teenagers with boundaries, clear standards and moral guidelines, and to be willing to openly discuss *why* parents believe these are important. But listening to why teenagers see things differently is also important. There is, however, a distinct difference between affirmation and approval. Parents can reassure teenagers that, while they are loved and unconditionally accepted, their choices or behaviour cannot be condoned. And if differences are discussed in a loving and guiding manner—devoid of judgment—the relationship between teenager and parent should not be damaged.

Q: Our son tells us that his friends' parents do, say, think this or that and therefore we should allow him to be the same. How can parents best deal with these situations?

A: It's interesting that in seeking to sidestep boundaries, we have probably all used this tactic at some time with varying degrees of success! Underlying these comments is generally a degree of subtle emotional blackmail: if their parents let them, why can't you? Don't you want to be good parents? Don't you care about me? The best way to approach this is to explain that you can't follow what other parents do and say if you don't believe it is the best thing. Explain that you will only ever do and say what *you* believe is the right thing to do. And be prepared to explain why you feel this way. This is teaching your teenager that you have morals you believe in and that you are prepared to stand by them even if this occasionally makes you unpopular. Some schools may teach philosophy, religious education, ethics and even values education in one way or another, but it is often at home that young people observe values, social and moral beliefs being lived out, and this is an essential aspect of every person's development and education.

Sonia, parent

When our son was keen to obtain his driving licence during his final year at school, it took a little persuasion for him to accept waiting the six months to the holidays before embarking on the test. He agreed (after his test!) that it would have been pretty distracting and additional tension to be learning to drive before exams.

Helping teenagers obtain a well-rounded education—making them life savvy

Don't shelter them from life. Make it commonplace to chat about topical issues and events—politics, refugees, the economy or world problems. Your teenager can learn invaluable skills from you—how to form an opinion, express their views with confidence and accept differences in opinion.

When your teenager hits tertiary education or the world of full-time work, they will be interacting with people from a diverse range of cultures, religions, people with different political and ethical beliefs, people with different sexual expectations and orientations. Your teenager is now at an age where they can decide who they will eventually vote for, who they will go out with, what they believe and where they want to go in life. The confidence they can gain through open and honest dialogue with you will be an invaluable support in all of this.

Jacob Rothfield, 18

My interest in theatre came from my grandma who from even my youngest years took me to musicals and plays. Knowledge about the theatre allowed me to enjoy English much more. (My English literature teacher would call me an 'intellectual'.)

Encouraging independence

I recently counselled a student who did not obtain a tertiary place at the end of high school. I managed to organise an interview for her at a university campus only to hear that she would be unable to attend the interview because her mother was working. This teenager had never taken public transport alone before. Horrified? I certainly was!

While this may be an extreme example, many students have never taken responsibility for choosing their own subjects, budgeting or completing application forms. Allow your teenager to gradually take on more responsibility. Small wins lead to larger wins. Be their adviser and supporter, but not their doer.

Despite all good intentions, if you do everything for teenagers, they will never learn. Make them responsible for their choice of subjects, friends, their room, a pet, cleaning up after their friends, mobile phone bills, clothes and personal possessions.

FAQ: Our daughter is completing her second-last year at high school and is still making excuses for not studying. How can we get her to take school seriously?

A: Unless your daughter decides she wants to do the study, it won't happen. This is a perfect time to help her identify those goals for the future that make the decision to work easier. Has she identified any careers that interest her? Does she have any general plans such as eventually travelling or working overseas? Even students with no idea of which career they want to pursue can have definite thoughts on what they want out of life—a great car, travel, loads of money, working with people, going into a challenging career. Sometimes looking ahead helps students gain focus and put in the hard work needed to achieve their goals.

It's also a good idea to check that your daughter isn't worrying about the final year at school and trying to forget about it by partying. I've heard many students say, 'This is our last chance to have fun.' Too much focus on the last year at school often filters down and affects younger students. In all of this, don't criticise her friends. They are irreplaceable at this stage of a teenager's life and having support from friends can help teenagers do better at school, especially in the final year.

Helping teenagers become decision-makers

Parents live in hope that their teenagers will make wise decisions when faced with the big choices. Will your teenager decide *not* to get into a car when the driver is obviously under the influence of alcohol? Will they decide to work hard at school rather than partying with friends? Every time you allow your teenager to experience the process of making a decision, you're preparing them to be able to make wise decisions about the bigger issues.

Practice makes perfect

Involve your teenager in discussing real-life decisions for the family. You may be considering a career change, moving house, purchasing a car, getting a dog or organising a family holiday. Ask them for their opinion.

Whoops . . .

Be prepared. They may make some 'bad' decisions but you won't always be around to protect them or pick them up. Ditch the lectures. Tell them everyone makes mistakes and what's important is to learn from them.

Back to the drawing board

When decisions don't work out as planned, model the art of re-evaluating a situation and making a positive move forward. Good old resilience training.

Peter Hillman, deputy principal

Dumbledore, in the conclusion of *Harry Potter and the Chamber of Secrets*, tells Harry that our choices reveal what we really are far more than our abilities. Dumbledore's wisdom is not just relevant at Hogwarts but for our children in the real world of the twenty-first century. It is the choices children make along the way that will determine their success—not intelligence, talents or background.

Only when children accept that they do have choices to make, do they begin to take responsibility for their actions. Parents can have a major affect on the way their children make these choices. I try to make time to talk to my children. Doing something together becomes a lubricant for discussion—walking the dog, kicking a football, a hit of tennis or even doing the dishes. This is particularly true for boys. It is amazing what will come out if it seems to be done in an informal way, without the heavy dialogue or too much eye contact.

Helping teenagers become opportunity-grabbers and opportunity-makers

Teenagers must be encouraged to be proactive and to seek out opportunities, from involvement in school activities to volunteering.

FAQ: I've heard many tertiary courses require students to have life experience and work experience as part of the selection process. My daughter is a good student but says she isn't interested in getting involved in any activities. What can we do about this?

A: Course selection officers certainly are looking at more than scores when selecting students. Here are a few practical suggestions to help out:

⊚ Encourage your daughter to investigate which courses require her to be interviewed or to complete detailed application forms outlining life experience, work experience and voluntary work. She will probably be surprised at what she discovers.

⊚ Any parent or student can also pick up the phone and contact the human resource manager/personnel manager in well-known companies and ask: 'What do you consider when selecting graduates? Is it true that impressive results alone are insufficient to land a graduate position?' Students are often blown away by the answers. Suddenly, getting a job at Maccas or volunteering during school holidays isn't such a bad idea after all!

⊚ Look through advertisements for graduate positions in newspapers or on internet employment sites so your teenager knows what to work towards. Invariably, requirements extend well beyond any particular qualification. Employers frequently expect applicants to demonstrate a *proactive approach to life*, leadership qualities, problem-solving ability, well-developed interpersonal skills, teamwork ability . . . These are extremely difficult to demonstrate in a job application unless students have become involved in aspects of life *apart from study*. Thousands of students never even reach the interview stage because their CVs look *ordinary*. I recently counselled a student with a Masters degree who was unable to crack an interview. He was a high achiever but had never allowed time to work, join clubs or become involved in anything except study. Big mistake! I suggested he travel overseas where he might successfully obtain employment or undertake voluntary work and part-time work to 'jazz up' his CV.

⊚ But don't alarm your daughter. It's never too late for students to work part-time, become involved in an area of interest or do voluntary work.

Encouraging teenagers to undertake part-time work

Why work?

⊚ Most teenagers have had some experience working before they leave high school.

⊚ Most tertiary students also tend to work part-time, and it will be more difficult for your son to obtain work at that point without previous experience.

⊚ Working enhances self-esteem, a sense of independence and self-confidence.

⊚ Work experience is highly regarded by course selection officers—it indicates a student is reliable, trustworthy, can accept responsibility, interact well with others (good interpersonal skills), has sound communication skills . . .

⊚ Employers can write references or act as referees if required by tertiary courses or future employers.

⊚ Working enables a young person to be more financially independent—this is a confidence boost in itself. It's also an opportunity to encourage a teenager to learn how to budget and save for a particular item.

⊚ Work provides an often-needed break from studies and an opportunity to widen their circle of friends so that they are not so reliant on school friends.

⊚ Often students who work are better organised than those who don't—provided they don't work too many hours.

Paul Laios, 18

Towards the end of my second-last year at school, I commenced casual employment with a computing company. I was surprised to be given a business card and direct line as soon as I joined and when I realised I would be paid commission on top of my salary, it seemed like icing on the cake. Going to work was more like a social experience for me. I made some good friends straight away. It was also enlightening to deal with people from a cross-section of the community and of varying ages.

Meeting interesting people, learning to work as part of a team and gaining insights into the business world has broadened my perspective and developed my interpersonal skills and confidence. Once I represented my company at a Home Entertainment Show. I've had two offers of full-time employment from clients, but I tell them I have to go to university. Most of all, working showed me that there is life beyond school. This definitely put the final year at school into perspective when my motto—much to my mother's distress—was 'Relax'. Working helped me mature and consequently prepared me for the interview process required for selection into some tertiary courses.

In essence

The best gift parents can give teenagers is to help them develop as thinking, discerning and enthusiastic individuals. This is the foundation that will enable them to go out and put their own stamp on the world.

Wisdom begins in wonder.

—Socrates

11

Approaching the final year with confidence

Not everything that can be counted counts, and not everything that counts can be counted.

—Albert Einstein

The final year of school is a stressful year for most parents and it's certainly the most daunting and stressful year most teenagers have faced up to that point in their lives. Not only do they have to focus on their studies, they have to contend with the media's attention on escalating scores and shortages of places in popular courses. Students frequently approach the year as though it is a 'life or death' struggle where there are winners and losers. Talk about stress city!

While there are practical strategies parents can use to support teenagers during their final year at school, it's essential to first get inside their heads and see things through their eyes. By understanding how they feel and what they fear, you can offer the right kind of support and reassurance.

All of the thoughts below have been expressed to me over and over again by students and parents—word for word.

It shouldn't be like this. Parents can help teenagers enormously by counterbalancing all the hype and helping to put the year into perspective.

What are teenagers saying and thinking?

- ◎ 'I'm scared of letting everyone down.'
- ◎ 'I'll never get a good enough score to go into . . .'
- ◎ 'If I mess this year up it's going to affect the rest of my life.'
- ◎ 'I couldn't face my family or friends if I didn't get a good score.'
- ◎ 'I just want the year to be over. I feel like running away.'
- ◎ 'You only get one chance at this. I can't stuff it up.'
- ◎ 'I wish my parents would back off and stop stressing about everything.'

What are parents saying and thinking?

- ◎ 'I don't know what to do, what to say or how to help my teenager this year. I'm scared of making things worse.'
- ◎ 'I'm worried that my teenager doesn't know what they want to do next year.'
- ◎ 'I don't know if my teenager is going well or not. I'm constantly worried.'

Ten ways to help teenagers approach their final year with confidence

1. Preserve their sanity

The most important role parents play in this year is to successfully strike a fine balance between encouraging teenagers to study hard while reinforcing the crucial message that the final year is not the be-all-and-end-all. As in fishing, there's the fine art of knowing when to tighten the line and when to leave well enough alone and wait patiently.

Ask your teenager how they feel about the year before they begin it and occasionally throughout the year to ensure they are feeling okay. As far as possible, try to stop the importance of the year from blowing out of all proportion. Don't radically alter the status quo. I know parents who exempt their teenagers from all housework duties as soon as they start the final year at school. There is a danger that teenagers read too much into this and begin to believe that the year is so important that life stops if it doesn't go well.

Maintaining a sense of *normality* is important. If everyone tiptoes around the house—'Quiiiiieeeet, they're studying!'—tension levels rise, not fall.

2. Look after yourself

You won't be able to help your teenager de-stress if you are frantic yourself. Don't allow yourself to be caught up in their anxiety. (Review 'Vital support for parents' in Chapter 2.)

3. Encourage a balanced approach

Most teenagers realise the final year requires their best organisation. Parents can help teenagers manage their workload and reduce other commitments if necessary. Talk to your teenager, but don't force them to drop all outside interests and friends. Students who do this rarely do as well as they could in the final year. Many show signs of burnout if they have no outlet for stress and no opportunity to switch off for a while.

Yanlo Yue, 18

In retrospect, I lived out my final year at school with no regrets. I had 'a life' as they say and tried not to always place my studies ahead of everything else. If I hadn't done this, I would've gone insane. All the outside activities and people I mixed with made me feel relaxed. My whole life was not dependent on my last year at school to make or break me. My enjoyment of the time seemed to result in even better grades than those who stressed over every piece of work and every exam. Halfway through the year I even engaged in job searches that have paid off these holidays . . .

Gordon Hope, 18

Surprisingly, I'm enjoying school more this year because I'm not involved in too many things. Last year I was involved in lots of things. I had the lead in the school musical, Victorian Youth Theatre every Sunday, cricket in the summer and footy in winter. I had training two nights a week. This year I haven't given up all of my interests but I've cut back a bit. If I dropped everything, I'd go mental.

4. Know and accept your teenager's academic capabilities

Most teenagers have a fairly good idea of their academic abilities. While most wouldn't be able to second-guess their eventual score, I certainly haven't come across too many D-average students scoring near perfect scores or straight-A students barely passing the final year. It's important for teenagers (and parents) to honestly align final score expectations to the teenagers' abilities.

Scores do not make or break your teenager's future prospects. The more I work with teenagers, the more I believe that anything is possible in good time. All kids mature and come into their own at different times. I see ex-students who struggled through school who are now impressing captains of industry. Some teenagers are not ready emotionally to do their best in the final year at school, but if they are not crushed or flattened, they will live to thrive academically another day. They may take the road less travelled and it may take a little longer, but it also might produce a more interesting (and successful) person down the track. Make sure your teenager doesn't feel unable to meet your expectations and survives the year with their self-esteem intact.

Adrian, 18

Study, study, that's all I hear. Even when I say I'm studying, dad says, 'Yeah, sure. Doesn't look like it.' I get the idea that he was a party animal when he was young and he doesn't want me to do the same. He says every generation should be stronger and smarter and more successful than the last. Every year when reports come in it's pretty bad. I used to say, 'Just let me have a good holiday and I'll do better next year'. I don't expect good holidays anymore. He wants too much from me. I don't want to do it anymore. I can't be bothered.

5. Believe the messages yourself

Unless you believe that your teenager's future *doesn't* hinge on that score at the end of the year, they generally won't believe it either. You might say the words but they'll see another message in your eyes or hear it in your voice. If you are convinced one year won't destroy a teenager's future, it will be so much easier to convince them.

6. Acknowledge that the year is tough for most students

Every parent wants their teenager to do well in the final year at school. Even if your teenager has cruised through the previous years, they may now be finding for the first time that work is challenging and need reassurance that this is *normal*. Most teenagers, regardless of their previous academic scores, feel that extra level of stress simply because this is the final year at school. Reassure your teenager that they have what it takes to complete the year.

7. Provide practical backup where possible

It's not a level playing field. Some kids have huge personal issues to deal with while others are lucky enough to sail through the year without a hitch. I've known students who had a whole host of little things go wrong, none of which qualified them for special consideration. Do whatever you can to give your teenager a leg up:

- A teenager's needs and moods can vary greatly from day to day. Try to judge when to push your teenager a little to study and when to stand back and give them space.
- There are some affordable crash courses and seminars on how to approach various subjects and study effectively. If your teenager shows interest in extra tuition, it may give them practical help and an added boost of confidence. Some students take turns attending various seminars and swap notes and insights with friends.
- Fetch and carry books and friends.
- Try to be more available at busy times—especially around exam periods—to drop them at school, pick them up or take them around to a friend's house. Time is a precious commodity for senior students.
- Help them investigate courses. There is an enormous amount of

reading required. I'll never forget the mother who showed me the list of computer courses she had investigated for her son. She knew so much about the courses I considered inviting her to my school as a guest speaker. She had listed the unique features of every course, major subjects, prerequisites required, electives available, career outcomes and entry scores. Granted, some teenagers would see this as interference, but many would welcome the time saved.

⊚ Look after your teenager! Students must be physically and emotionally fit to do their best in the final year. Year after year, I see some students who are emotionally drained. It's counterproductive to study until 3.00 a.m. day after day. Students end up falling asleep in class or missing school. Students need adequate sleep, a good diet (rather than being *on* a diet) and enough exercise to blow away some of the cobwebs.

Peter Hillman, deputy principal and parent

Senior exam pressure is very real. We tried to relieve it as much as possible. The family made sacrifices. There was a parent around before each exam—a walk together around the block worked for us— getting some head space before being dropped at the examination centre. When our daughter found it hard to sleep in her final year, we donated the study for her schoolwork. This left her bedroom as a refuge, a space away from work, and insomnia was less of a problem.

Paul Laios, 18

My parents have always been supportive through school. Their confidence in me never faltered even when I had bouts of doubt about getting the score I needed for my tertiary preferences. If I ever looked uncertain this would send my mother into a frenzy of motivational rhetoric. In hindsight their contribution helped me get through the year. Their interest and concern made me focus on my long-term goals, as I was prone to easy distraction. They cautioned me to balance work, school and social commitments, including my involvement with a local Youth Reference Group. Being on this committee meant a quick dash home from school on Tuesday afternoons to eat, change and be at a meeting by four o'clock. Dad, like a loyal chauffeur, would be there promptly at six to take me home. My involvement in this community service helped me fulfil some criteria that selection panels seek in candidates. We discussed youth issues, developed group presentations to council and held forums on issues such as drugs and alcohol. I always felt secure in the knowledge that nothing was too much trouble for my parents. My mother often stayed up late to keep me company while I plodded through mounds of subject material. Their encouragement helped me cope with the stress of meeting deadlines and I think that in the end, they were more relieved than I was when the final exam was over.

Anna Kelsey-Sugg, 21

My parents took a pretty active role in my final year at school. They read the texts I had to read and hired the films for us to watch. They were constantly tearing out articles from journals or papers that might relate to one of my subjects and pulling out old books of theirs—anything that might help. Talking about what I was studying was a huge help. I could study alone for hours about Napoleon and the French Revolution for example, but talking helped me clarify ideas. In third year uni this is still a study method I rely on. My parents are always prepared to sit down and 'talk school'.

8. Encourage them to get support from their friends, form study groups and network

Support from friends in the final year at school can make an enormous difference. They provide that irreplaceable 'we're in this together and we'll get through this together' camaraderie.

Friends can also be valuable resources. Most students have friends attending other schools. I've known students from various schools who have agreed to exchange their study notes, handouts from teachers and corrected essays. Reading comments from teachers at other schools can provide additional insights into texts being covered. This gives students extra confidence, especially in preparing for final exams.

9. Allow them to follow their heart

Support your teenager by showing your interest in courses and careers but always allow them to make the final decision. I vividly recall the student who was too scared to tell his father he wanted to be an interior designer. 'Dad's a doctor, my two uncles are doctors and I'm to do the same. That's the way it goes. I asked dad if I should consider other careers and he said not to waste time. He says I'll thank him one day and that I'm so lucky to have a practice to join when I graduate.' This is one of the few occasions I've hoped a student wouldn't receive the score to get a place in medicine. When I see ex-students in situations like this a few years down the track, they generally fall into two groups. Some are finally doing what *they* want to do but rarely have a close relationship with their families. Others are still dutifully engaged in careers set out for them at birth, but their eyes are not lit up the way the eyes of young people should be. I tell these students to watch the Hollywood movie *While You Were Sleeping* and to have the courage to tell their parents what they really want to do.

I also know students who were promised impressive gifts (cars, holidays) if they successfully obtained a place at a particular university. Another student told me his parents would leave the room if he tried to explain why he wanted to be a social worker rather than an engineer. I'll never forget the student who was promised a car if she made it into one of several prestigious universities and a dog if she didn't. She got the dog and they are both very happy. Not surprisingly, she has a distant relationship with her parents. Cute dog though!

Make sure your teenager:

- isn't pressured by the advice of well-meaning relatives, friends or media articles. Some teenagers even tell me they must sacrifice certain careers because they have heard employment is impossible to obtain. Going into a course they are passionate about is not 'risky' or foolish: there will always be jobs for the passionate souls;
- is familiar with courses and tertiary institutions. The same course can vary at different institutions. Encourage them to contact course advisers and people working in various careers and arrange to visit them for advice;

- knows that the best institution is the one offering the course that suits their interests, not the one some people say has the best reputation. Institutions vary in size, atmosphere and sometimes even teaching style. Students who investigate thoroughly maximise their chances of feeling 'at home';
- isn't choosing a course because *you* have praised it so much they feel handcuffed to your hopes and dreams. Sometimes, even unintentionally, we influence choices teenagers make. If their heart isn't in it, it's a risky choice.

One's real life is often the life that one does not lead.

—Oscar Wilde

Yanlo Yue, 18

I've heard some pretty ridiculous things. Some of my mates' parents truly believe that anything below an almost perfect score is a complete failure. Every student is scared of disappointing someone or not living up to expectations: themselves, parents, teachers, society and so on. My friend has a mother who's a dentist. In her (well-intentioned) efforts to get her daughter to study dentistry, the condition was that if she didn't study dentistry she would need to pay rent to live at home. Talk about pressure!

Jacob Rothfield, 18

My parents never dictated my activities or interests, yet they did not leave it all to me either. At high school I didn't know what I wanted to be or do. At one stage I thought I wanted to be a businessman, another time a computer person, and now an inventor/scientist. Even though my parents put my future in my hands, they never stopped suggesting things that could 'broaden my horizon' or break a prejudice. I'm very lucky they have this sort of non-dictated but open-minded approach to nurturing my interests.

> **Professor John Catford, dean, Health and Behavioural Sciences, Deakin University**
>
> Many students don't think enough about why they are choosing a particular course or university. They feel pressure from parents and friends when deciding where to study, and too often make the wrong choices as a result.

10. Say you are proud of efforts rather than just glowing results

Believe me, this is the best way to help your teenager look the final year in the eye and give it their best.

Five essential messages teenagers need to hear from parents

1. 'The final year at school is not the most important year of your life!'

One year can't destroy a teenager's life chances *unless they believe it can*. Given too much importance, it becomes a miserable and stressful time for everyone, and over-worried students rarely perform at their best. Help your teenager get the year into perspective.

> **Amy Boughen, 17**
>
> What's the final year at school feel like? Like I've been climbing a mountain for so long and now I'm finally at the top . . . but it's a cliff with a long way down. I'm either going to fall or make it out. What worries me most is that I might not do as well as I want to and I'll let down all the people who have helped me out. This is how many students feel. We're all hoping to make it out alive.

Adriana Ong, 20, currently completing a Bachelor of Business (Strategic and Financial Management)

During my last year of school I sort of gave up. I was tired of studying after a continuous thirteen years. I had put a great deal of pressure on myself to do my best and to make my parents feel that all of their hard-earned money for tutors was finally getting the results they deserved. I ruined any chances of getting into some universities as I mucked up my subject choices. I did subjects that my heart clearly wasn't in and received disappointing grades.

I wasn't at all impressed by my final results and I felt as though I had failed myself. I cried for days on end. It was a horrible time. My friends and parents supported me and motivated me throughout the whole process. At first my parents were a bit disappointed with my score, but they have continued to love and support me. Although I initially thought it was the end of the world not receiving a good score, it clearly isn't. As mum always says, it doesn't matter where you go to get your education—it's what you make of it.

2. 'Results are overrated! If you don't do well at school, you're not "stuffed"!'

It's disturbing that even early high-school students are starting to worry about results and entry scores. A student approached me at the start of this year. 'Miss, can I ask you something? What do you think scores for university will be when I get there?' He looked so *little*. And, sure enough, he had been at high school for the grand total of one week! I must have looked shocked. 'It's a bad answer Miss, isn't it? I can take it.' I was thinking: 'Why aren't you out kicking a ball?'

We must temper student anxiety: 'Just do your best. There are endless options ahead of you and you should be looking forward to next year.' Year after year, the most stressed senior students I counsel are those whose parents have extremely high expectations. Students who are afraid of taking home their results often can't achieve their best. If the bar is set too high, students subconsciously give up or fall to pieces in exam situations.

I see escalating numbers of senior students on anti-depressants, looking as though they have the worries of the world on their young shoulders. I don't know any parent who would exchange their teenager's peace of mind, mental health or self-esteem for an impressive score, yet all these are at risk unless the year is put into perspective.

Regardless of results, there are good courses for students with scores from the lowest to the highest. Some students perform better at the tertiary level than those with much higher tertiary entrance scores. What counts in the long run is self-belief, determination and the knowledge that support from home is a given, not something only earned by particular results. Does your teenager know they have your unconditional support?

Anna Kelsey-Sugg, 21

In my last year at high school, a 'motivational' speaker spoke to my year level and his advice for doing well was to write on your desk the score 99 and look at it every day while studying. This, he said, would imprint the high score in your mind and make you work towards it. At the time I wasn't nearly as appalled as I should have been. People around me were telling me my score at the end of the year was the most important thing in my life so far. I'm lucky my parents did not build up my final year at high school to be the BIGGEST ONE EVER. Instead they constantly reminded me that finishing school meant the start of a whole lot of exciting choices.

Wai Yin Lo, 22

I wish I'd known your score isn't as important as it's made out to be. All we heard was SCORES, SCORES, SCORES. I'd like to tell students that if they do manage to get a high score they should make sure they boast about it because a year later it will have absolutely no meaning. And those who don't get a high score shouldn't worry. There are heaps of opportunities out there.

'M.L.S', 21

Things started to go terribly wrong as I approached the higher years of high school. The game changed. The aim was to get the highest possible score, holding nothing back. Morals no longer counted. Paying to have essays and assignments written was the norm. I'm not sure how I got through the last year. It's all a blur. I became very anxious and couldn't sleep. I saw the school counsellor who referred me to a psychiatrist. At the time I thought I was the only one having problems but speaking to friends now, many were on some form of anti-depressant. Which makes you wonder what for! I finished school and went rather well. I applied for a range of courses in the music field as well as Education and Arts. I was accepted on the spot at all three music university auditions and offered an Arts degree too. I accepted a place in a specialist music university and three years later have yet to regret the decision.

3. 'There are many pathways to get where you want to go.'

Students who have all their hopes pinned on getting into one particular course at one particular university are generally setting themselves up for a stressful year. Students need lots of contingencies.

Pathways students should be aware of

- University is *not* the best option for all students. Students should consider the unique benefits of both university and all other technical and vocational training courses and select the course most suited to their interests. They need to know that their parents see all courses as valuable options.
- TAFE (Technical and Further Education) courses often give students credit into many university courses.
- There are mid-year intakes into some university and TAFE courses for students who have missed out on a place.
- Some universities offer one-year preparatory courses (generally called a Diploma of Foundation Studies) that students can complete and then use to move into various degree courses (see Chapter 10).
- Teenagers sometimes benefit from working or travelling after completing high school so that they can regain focus and find what they are interested in before beginning tertiary study. With the benefit of life experience, they often outperform students entering tertiary study straight from school.

- Short courses at TAFE allow students to build up a portfolio of skills and knowledge. These can be completed while working full- or part-time and help students gain full-time places in TAFE or university courses.
- Most universities offer *single subjects* from a wide variety of courses. Regardless of high-school results, students can enrol in a few subjects and, with good results, reapply to be accepted into a university course. Fees for these must be paid up front, but students can help pay for these by working part-time. This is also a great way for them to keep busy and maintain a network of friends.
- Apprenticeships and traineeships are available in many areas.
- Courses at university campuses in rural areas are easier to obtain places in than those in major cities.

The most important task parents have is to remind teenagers there is a big exciting world out there full of possibilities and a low score is small potatoes in comparison. With support, students can pick themselves up and forge ahead in amazing ways—*provided their self-esteem is protected.*

There are many paths to the top of the mountain, but the view is always the same.

—Chinese proverb

4. 'You don't have to know what you want to be at the end of school!'

Few teenagers leave school with that definitive 'Ahha that's what I want to be when I grow up' feeling.

It's common for teenagers to be undecided about what they want 'to be'. Ironically, many students who believe they know what they want to become change their minds once into tertiary study. And this applies even to students who have thoroughly investigated courses and careers. Students who 'get it right' first go are often just very lucky.

Students who are unsure of a career often choose generalist courses such as Arts, Commerce or Science and select subjects they enjoy. After all, education is not merely for one's 'career', but to enjoy the whole process of becoming informed, aware and thinking members of the community. These degrees also allow students to specialise and gain skills that lead on to a huge variety of careers. Help your teenager become familiar with how tertiary courses work and the flexibility of many courses.

Aylin Eser, 20

In my final year at school I didn't really know why I was studying. I had no direction. It was a horrible feeling. It was as though I walked through the whole year with an invisible blindfold on. I knew that if I achieved good marks I was likely to get a place at university. However, because I didn't know what I wanted to study, I couldn't even experience the joy of imagining myself in that position. It was a frightening year.

Sarah Wilson, journalist

They say the death of a loved one, a long-term relationship bust-up and moving house are up there as some of the most stressful moments in a person's life. I have experienced all three (several times over) and feel it only fair to add choosing a career path to the list. Little else has come close to matching the existential angst I experienced at the end of high school working out what I was going to 'be' when I grew up. I spent lunchtimes poring over career books in the library trying to negotiate the best path for my future. Forever the kid who over-researched her assignments, I rang law firms, naturopaths (and, at one stage, a horse trainer) and asked complete strangers if they liked their jobs and whether they'd recommend their line of work. In the end, mainly from sheer exhaustion, I wound up enrolling in an Arts/Law degree because that's what you did when you got the grades.

Like most of Generation X, I was told that the only way to get a job was to get high grades in school and a place in a solid university course (read: law, accounting, science—none of this 'diploma in motivational water therapy' stuff). It was also drummed into me—by my parents and teachers—that the decision I made at that point would determine the career conveyor belt I was to ride for the rest of my working life. It wasn't their fault, but their advice was misguided.

So what should young people be told now? Well, for starters there is no such thing as a linear career path. Today's jobs market is so volatile that most of us must weave a crooked path from career to career as jobs arise. To this end, students should never panic if they find themselves meandering down a career/ study path that doesn't entirely suit them. There is always the time and opportunity to shift course. In fact, many employers encourage it.

Second, it doesn't matter what you study when you leave high school, so long as you learn something and are enriched by the experience. Employers today are often simply after evidence of a young person's ability to apply themselves to something, whether it be a Law degree or a diploma in flower arranging. I started out in Law, then swapped to an Arts degree, completing part of my studies in America as an exchange student. Then, after several years in the workforce, I did a TAFE course in professional writing. In hindsight, extracurricular activities throughout my university years counted for far more than my grades. I did a political internship, was involved in student politics and wrote for the student newspaper. I can say with absolute certainty that not once have I ever been asked to explain my uni grades. I have, however, been repeatedly asked in interviews to outline 'my experiences' over the years.

More than a decade after leaving high school, I found myself working as a feature writer and columnist and I am now an associate editor of a women's magazine. No TAFE or university course could have directly prepared me for these jobs. I am where I am now as a result of an accumulation of experiences and jobs. Put simply, I had to define my path for myself, which wasn't easy, but it has certainly paid off.

5. 'Do your best . . . that's all we want.'

Teenagers need to believe that their parents don't have unrealistic expectations of them. One of the most common laments I hear from students is that parents are never satisfied. I'll never forget the student who was so afraid of his parents seeing his final results that he had generated a new certificate with a higher score. His parents dragged him up to see me, as they were suspicious when he didn't receive a tertiary offer despite his good score. Privacy legislation (to say nothing of an overwhelming feeling of sympathy for this young person's situation) prevented me from verifying that the document was false. Eventually, however, he broke down and cried as he confessed the truth. It is an awful experience to sit back and watch a young person who is genuinely afraid of their parents.

Although they may hide it, most teenagers desperately want to please their parents. Believing that they might disappoint parents is a heavy load for a young person to carry. Make sure your teenager knows that you love them regardless of their results.

More than any other year, the final school year is when many parents are afraid to 'stuff up'. I've had parents cry while telling me they feel constantly overwhelmed. It's important to get support from other parents and teachers. So here are some of the questions I hear over and over again from parents and some of the advice that I have found does work for students.

FAQs

Q: Our daughter appears to be very stressed in her last year at school even though we have a great relationship with her and have never put pressure on her. What can we do?

A: Ironically, I've seen many students who have fantastic parents feeling as stressed as students who don't have good relationships with their parents. These students tell me that their parents are so wonderful that they can't bear the thought of letting them down. One student said to me, 'I'm scared of seeing my results. Mum and dad have done everything for me. I have to do well for them.' *Ask* your daughter how she feels and what worries her. *Tell* her that, whatever her results are, you won't crack up, or be disappointed in her. Students talk about all of these possibilities. Reassure her that there are fantastic courses that don't require high scores and help her identify some.

Q: Is TAFE really okay?

A: Absolutely! TAFE is not for the dropouts. If only I had a dollar for every time I've answered this question. Take your teenager along to an Open Day. You'll both be impressed.

Professor Richard Teese, Post-compulsory Education and Training, University of Melbourne

TAFE courses offer important benefits to school leavers. They have good career outcomes and lead to higher earnings. From a learning perspective, they offer small-group teaching (instead of mass lectures in which students are not infrequently lost), better supervision of student work, a more practical emphasis on teaching and opportunities for an industry practicum. Student satisfaction with TAFE courses is high and completing a diploma gives students credit into a degree. Choosing this path helps students consolidate their learning so that when they do enter university they have a greater prospect of success. TAFE programs are not simply stepping-stones to higher education. Both in Australia and overseas, they provide direct access to employment. Finally, they are a lot less expensive. Students who do not take a serious look at TAFE courses and include at least one in their list of preferences are taking a big, unnecessary risk. Will they be one of the 29 per cent of university students who never finish their degree? Will they be one of the many who complete university only to find they need to go to TAFE to gain more specific job skills and preparation?

Dr Barry Golding, School of Education, University of Ballarat

There are at least three times as many people moving from university to TAFE as there are from TAFE to university. About half are university graduates and half of those didn't fully complete a degree. The modern notion of lifelong learning is encouraging university graduates to study further at TAFE in a bid to stay ahead of the pack.

Anna Masters, 20

In hindsight, I am quite relieved that I didn't attend university straight after school, as I wasn't a very confident person then. Even my first term of TAFE was daunting. Although TAFE is smaller than a university campus, it's amazing how many times I got lost. I missed out on Orientation Week so it took me an entire first semester to find the canteen. I was too embarrassed to ask someone for directions.

TAFE gives you that first step into post-high school education without feeling overwhelmed with the mass of students, buildings and campus size most universities have. I've just completed my TAFE course and I'm very happy that I have already been accepted into a university degree in Professional Writing.

Q: How can we make our son consider sensible careers? He's a gifted student but insists he wants to be a plumber.

A: Support your son if that's what he wants to be. It is far better having a happy plumber in the family than an unhappy doctor/lawyer/whatever! An added bonus is that there is a worldwide shortage in most trade areas and the financial rewards are fantastic too.

No one should look down on careers in the trade area. They are great for kids who prefer working with their hands and who don't like the idea of working in an office. Some of the happiest and most successful ex-students I know are working in various trades. *Students should always let their passion, not scores, guide them.*

Q: Our daughter has had a part-time job for the past two years. Now that she's in the last year of high school, should we make her give this up and concentrate more on her studies?

A: It's never a good idea to make a student do anything. It's always better to help them evaluate a situation or reach a compromise so that they feel they 'own' the decision. Many senior students cut back on the hours they work but maintain their jobs. Working can be a fantastic de-stressor for students. For a few hours they can forget about school and just be a young person having fun and interacting with other staff and customers. Many course selection officers also look favourably on students who have work experience.

Anthony Lio, 17

The thing I've learnt since leaving school is that you don't have to follow any set path. I got into a double degree in Commerce/Law but didn't feel it was quite for me. Even though some of my best friends were doing the same course, we barely saw each other. Uni is a big place and sometimes you feel like a small figure drifting amongst the crowd. So, rather than continue down a path of uncertainty and discontent, I decided to defer. Many people question you when you defer. 'Give it a longer go', 'Are you sure? It's silly to give up.' There's pressure to keep doing something you don't feel right about; pressure to fit into the 'norm' of graduating from high school, going to uni, getting married and so forth. After deferring I took some time out and got a job at a pharmacy. It has made me more independent, taught me how to take care of myself, and given me valuable life experience. I'm not sure what I'll eventually do about uni, but at least I've got time to think about things.'

[Anthony worked for a year before returning to a new university course. He's now 21 and in his third year of dentistry. Anthony is enjoying dentistry and still says the year he deferred was one of the best years of his life.]

Skye Koehne, 19

By taking a year off before going to uni, I was able to work my thoughts out. It made me de-stress, have some fun and organise my life. I also worked and saved some cash for a car and holidays. When I do return to studies I will be clear-headed and able to give schooling my full concentration and commitment. I think the year off also helped with my personal maturity. Life's too short to waste time on courses I wasn't mentally prepared for. I had a chance to decide what I want, not what everyone else wants for me. Now I feel I can go to uni, actually enjoy it and get somewhere in my life. Taking a break helps you put everything into perspective.

[Skye has just enrolled in a TAFE Marketing Diploma and loves it. She intends to transfer to university at the end of her course and knows her degree will be significantly shortened because of the credits she will receive. She has a huge smile on her face.]

Rowan Winsemius, 18

After spending thirteen years of my life in a school, the last thing I wanted was to spend the next three or four in a university. I didn't work exceptionally hard in the last year at school but the cumulative effect of the previous twelve years caught up with me. I needed a break. I think every school leaver deserves a decent holiday. I figured the end of high school presented the perfect opportunity to go travelling so I started working part-time in my mid-teens and full-time as soon as my final exams were over at the end of high school. My venture into full-time work was a great experience. I learnt business skills, earned good money for my trip and had a great time. I'm about to head off to do ten weeks' voluntary work in Namibia with an international charity. I don't want to do the usual sort of touristy things. I want to get off the beaten track and also know that at least I'm doing something useful in a struggling area of the world.

Update . . . Rowan, 19

Travelling and doing voluntary work was fantastic. Not every 19-year-old guy can say they've built part of a school in a desert community in Namibia or had the opportunity to work 50 metres from elephants for three weeks. The sense of satisfaction was huge. Since arriving home, I've changed what I'm studying at uni and have a more definite plan of where I want to be in five or ten years' time rather than just guessing. I've also got some great elephant and cheetah photos!

Q: How can we make our son take the last year at school more seriously? His sister was much more organised and did very well.

A: Sometimes students who are blasé about study—especially boys—are hiding their fears and need reassurance. Fooling around provides a convenient excuse if their results are not great. It's important that your son doesn't feel obliged to match or better his sister's results. I've heard countless students lamenting the fact that all of their siblings did very well at school and they feel the pressure is on not to let the team down. Every child is different and should never feel obliged to measure up to any other.

Casually ask your son how he feels about the year. You may also have to consider the possibility that he is simply not ready to get into serious study at this stage. Cheer up! Many teenagers change dramatically in the next year or even a few months out of school and return to study 'switched on' and able to produce great results.

Q: My daughter admits she has 'stuffed around' and now regrets it. There are only three months to go till her exams. We don't know how to help her or what to say.

A: Reassure her that it's almost never too late! I have seen students turn things around and produce amazingly good work in the last few months. Advise her to speak to teachers immediately—they are generally more than willing to help students who are genuinely prepared to give the exams a real go. Tell her that every day counts and to make the most of every day. Advise her to organise a study plan for each day or week. Most of all, tell her that you will support her and that you are proud of her.

Q: My daughter has always excelled at school but now that she's in her final year, she's beginning to doubt her abilities. How can I help?

A: Even high achievers need reassurance because they tend to place high expectations on themselves. Sometimes, as the work gets harder, even previously excellent students may begin to struggle. Some may even start to feel like 'failures' when their results dip only a fraction. And students who have never experienced what it's like to fail don't always have as much resilience as others facing final exams (they've never known failure therefore never had to cope with it). Their confidence can be easily shaken at the first sign of a 'bad' result. If this happens, parents need to step in and help them through these confidence-shaking attacks.

One student recently told me that she had always done very well at school and was afraid her luck might run out in the final exams. She spoke of 'blowing everything when it really counts'. I reminded her that it had nothing to do with luck, adding that she had developed excellent study techniques over the years and that she had actually listened to teachers and followed their advice right throughout the year. She was in a strong position to do well. I also reminded her that there are more important things than high scores and that many good courses do not require the highest scores. These are the messages all students need to hear and they have the most impact when they come from parents.

Melike Ozcagli, 21

Parents need to let their children make 'mistakes'. 'Mistakes' make you aware of what you don't want, bringing you closer to what you do want. My parents didn't put huge pressure on me during my last year at school, but I still felt stressed because I couldn't choose between fashion design and primary teaching. I was so confused. I ended up in a fashion course and even completed it. Although I liked fashion, I realised more and more that I enjoyed caring for others. I'm now confident that I want to become a primary teacher. If I'd gone straight into a primary teaching course out of high school, I wouldn't have been as prepared or as confident. I would have also had a question mark in my head about fashion and wasting my creative streak. Now I know that I can use my creativity to inspire children and make their schooling more exciting.

I couldn't have known any of this at 18. Students and parents should relax because you don't have to make the 'right' choice the first time. Every experience gives you a better understanding of yourself and your qualities.

Q: We have heard end of school celebrations can be rather wild. Should we allow our daughter to participate?

A: Completing high school is an important milestone and teenagers should be encouraged to celebrate it. Talk openly to your daughter about your fears of the dangerous antics that can occur and make sure she knows that your only concern is that she is safe. Teenagers often measure up well when they are trusted and at some point this is all we can do—trust that they have taken in some of the values and beliefs we have instilled in them throughout their life. Banning a teenager from celebrations can sometimes backfire, as they find other ways to prove a point—'You can't stop me!'

In addition to the teenagers' celebrations, it's great to celebrate your daughter's completion of high school as a family. This is saying that you are proud of her for having completed high school and takes the focus away from results for a while. After results arrive, regardless of the level of success, make sure your daughter knows you are proud of her.

In essence

Like it or not, the final year at school will always be stressful for students and parents. You can, however, ensure that your teenager has the right information and hears the right messages from you—messages that lift them up and allow them to do their best knowing that you are right there supporting them.

All students have good and bad days. Your job is to pick them up on the bad days and tell them you believe in them. To summarise, these things will help them cope:

Energy boosters/de-stressors for students:

- good food, adequate sleep;
- exercise/sport—students need *energy* to do their best;
- a balance of study and interests;
- a family celebration when a significant piece of work is completed (not only when results arrive);
- practical help from parents;
- time with friends;
- short breaks during study time rather than long slogs;
- occasionally a complete break away from study to recharge energy levels—a study-free weekend;
- knowing that there are an endless array of great courses that *don't* require high scores;
- positive messages and reassurance from home;
- believing that the final year at school *isn't* capable of wrecking their entire life.

There is nothing like a dream to create the future.

—Victor Hugo

12

Beyond the school gates

The object of education is to prepare the young to educate themselves throughout their lives.

—Robert M. Hutchins

Although teenagers frequently scream delight at completing high school, leaving behind the security of the known and stepping out into the world beyond isn't easy even for the most confident teenagers. A certain sadness and apprehension, however well concealed, often accompanies the excitement and the partying. It can be very scary out there. Many teenagers feel lonely and lost as they face the dawning realisation that leaving school is a step into adulthood.

All big transitions involve a certain sense of loss. The transition from school to the world beyond is one of the greatest transitions we all face at a time when we are all relatively ill-equipped to face it. Many teenagers enter tertiary institutions or workplaces where they have few or no friends. It's important for parents to be supportive and observe signs that their teenager may occasionally be feeling overwhelmed during this time. In a recent study of school leavers, 81 per cent most often cited parents, family and other significant adults as being their main source of information influencing their work and study choices.[1] They do listen and they do need support.

I've asked hundreds of students about to complete high school how they feel about the future. Answers reflect both excitement and a growing concern with the uncertainty of the world they face.

How do teenagers feel about finishing high school?

Today's world is unquestionably competitive, fast-paced and very uncertain. Against this backdrop, the years from ages 18 to 25 are monumentally significant ones for young people. These are the years when they're working out answers to the big questions in life, 'completing' identity formation, forming important personal relationships and searching for their own unique niche in life. They are literally finding their way.

They are excited about:
- having more *freedom* and independence;
- being able to make more decisions;
- being seen as adults.

They worry about:
- failing at the tertiary level/work;
- not being good enough;
- losing touch with friends from school;
- not being able to make new friends;
- not knowing what they want to do in the future;
- not getting a job.

I see countless ex-students who believe they are the only ones who feel bewildered and lost. They're afraid their parents will see them as weak or immature if they share these feelings, so some slide into depression. You can't assume that, once your teenager is safely into a job or tertiary course, the danger period is over. Many teenagers sail through high school only to come 'unstuck' when they step beyond the school gates. A staggering number fail at university and TAFE, or are unable to adjust successfully to workplace demands. Research indicates almost one in five university students drop out after their first year of study;[2] while a recent federal government report shows that the national average drop-out rate from award courses is currently 18.5 per cent.[3]

What can parents do?

You can help your teenager enormously during these crucial years. Let's look at the major hurdles teenagers face outside the school gates and some practical strategies you can use to help with their transition.

These are some of the issues you may find yourself helping your teenager through:
- results;
- no tertiary offer;
- dissatisfaction with the tertiary offer;
- helping your teenager adjust to first-year university or other post-high school studies;
- full-time employment blues—school to work, TAFE/university to work;
- finding their place in the world.

What can you do if your teenager is disappointed with their results?

Regardless of their results—*celebrate!* They have completed their high school education!

Many teenagers feel they have 'failed' even though they have successfully obtained a tertiary place because that place is not at one of the so-called 'best' institutions. It's not a good mindset to begin tertiary life with! Even if you are disappointed yourself, don't let on. Put on a brave face and move on with your teenager. There's nothing you or your teen can do about the results now. How you react and 'use' the results makes all the difference in the world. This is the time to move gently into damage control mode. *Tell them you are proud of them.* Tell them their first course is *the beginning* not the end point in their post-school education.

I've seen more devastated students than I care to remember. In every case, the primary concern of these students has been what their parents will think of them! Don't let your teenager doubt your belief in them for a second.

What can parents do if their teenager receives no tertiary offer?

Another damage-control situation! Teenagers (and parents) need to believe this is not the end of the world! Act quickly and help your teenager recover from this blow:

- Get them out of bed (many students do literally hide under the covers).
- Encouragement, encouragement, encouragement! There are great courses out there for every student, regardless of their results.
- They should be able to return to their high school for careers advice. If not . . .
- Contact every university and TAFE institute. Visit them and identify courses your teenager can gain entry to. They may have to travel a little further than they had hoped, but *a good course is a good course!*
- Ask about part-time options available at university and TAFE and courses starting mid-year, as these are often easier to gain entry to.
- Often single subjects can be completed from university courses. Although these must be paid for up-front, students can work part-time while studying to help cover costs. I've seen many students seize this opportunity, experience great success and transfer into full-time university studies.
- Investigate bridging courses or short courses that will enhance chances of mid-year entry.
- Investigate traineeships that can lead on to further study at TAFE or university: hospitality, IT, business and retail, sport, etc.
- Many students take a year off to work and travel before deciding what the next step into full-time study or work will be.

What can you do if your teenager is unhappy with their tertiary offer?

Tell them that many students who obtain good results transfer into other courses after completing a year at university or TAFE. I've known some who have even transferred after one semester. Many students also officially defer their course and take time off to think things through. But they must inform the institution of their plans rather than drift away and lose their place.

Helping your teenager adjust to first–year university/TAFE

Unable to adjust to the new demands and freedom, many students do not survive first year at university. Even well-prepared students may find the first few weeks and even months a lonely and alienating experience. Most ex-students I counsel admit feeling embarrassed to tell their parents how unhappy they are. These are often the students who swallowed the message that the final year at school was the hardest of their life. They are shocked to be having problems in the 'real world' and believe that admitting it shows they cannot cope with it.

What students need to do well at the tertiary level

A different kind of parental support

The most important task parents have at this point is to help teenagers stand on their own feet. Letting go isn't easy but if teenagers are ever to become independent, they must be allowed to test their wings—even if this means 'failing' occasionally. Accept that, while you will always be in your teenager's life, you will increasingly become the background supporter as they take on greater responsibility for their life and decisions. In other words, *let them fly*. Believe me, they'll thank you for it. When I ask students what they are most looking forward to about tertiary study, most mention having more freedom and being treated as adults.

Encourage your teenager to start making important decisions and taking increasing responsibility for their life. Each taste of *being in control* empowers teenagers and prepares them for bigger responsibilities and decisions ahead.

Friends!

Loneliness is one of the most common problems facing students who don't take the initiative to socialise. As one researcher states, 'Social transition underpins a successful academic transition to university . . . not having friends [makes] the whole process of transition to university more difficult, whilst having friends [helps] students to settle in quickly and make progress with their studies.'[4] Many ex-students have told me they feel 'stupid' about feeling lonely and would never dream of mentioning this to their friends or family. They believe they're the only one feeling lost.

- Encourage your teenager to become involved in university activities. Participating in Orientation Week is a great way to make new friends.
- Remind them that they must be *proactive* in order to make friends—perhaps asking a fellow student for a coffee or volunteering to join a committee. Share your own experiences of making friends in new workplaces.

○ *Remind them to keep in contact with high-school friends and not to cut ties!* This is especially important for teenagers who find themselves in courses or institutes with few or no friends from their high school days.

Wai Yin Lo, 22

I wasn't involved in much during my first year at uni. It was a foreign, lonely and even boring place for me. I didn't know who to turn to for help. In second year I stumbled on a volunteer Student Leadership Program. This opened up a huge range of opportunities for me and has given me lots of confidence. Initially I only hoped to gain better teamwork and communication skills but I organised orientation events, joined committees and even became president of a sports club. I've also helped organise and lead ski weekends and dolphin swims for students and have met a fantastic range of interesting people. It wasn't until I did all of these things that I discovered uni might be fun after all.

Heaps of knowledge

Students should visit institutions and thoroughly investigate courses *before* arriving on the doorstep. They must know what is expected and where to get support. Do lots of investigation yourself and even visit institutions with your teenager. Best of all, discuss everything with them.

Professor John Catford, dean, Health and Behavioural Sciences, Deakin University

Making the transition from school to university, it's helpful for students to use the same process they would use planning a trip overseas, with customs, money, dangers and how to protect yourself from risks . . . Where do you want to go, why do you want to go there and what do you want to achieve?

A willingness to seek advice and help

Many students are unwilling to discuss their concerns with anyone.[5] Give the clear message that going into tertiary education is exciting but involves a *steep learning curve*. Asking for help and advice is *common* and the smart thing to do! Ensure they know about all the support services available on campus.

Ability to work independently

Many courses have low contact hours, with requirements for students' presence in classes far from full-time. Students who can't research and study without a high degree of supervision or contact with staff often come unstuck. For many, this is a strange and even lonely experience. Encourage your teenager to develop friendship/study groups within various subjects. This enables students to help each other and keep on track.

Self-discipline

Distractions are *everywhere* and no one reminds students about work, takes the roll or checks on their progress. Students must be able to balance studies with social activities and often with part-time work.

Encourage your teenager to have a clear picture of when assignments and exams are due. Generally all dates are given at the start of a semester, but it's easy for students to forget these and fall behind. Also encourage them to actually attend classes. Many students skip classes for weeks on end because they're having so much fun.

Ability to adjust to academic expectations and teaching styles

Students must learn what is expected in a tertiary-style essay. They should know that tutorials are there to provide a more individual setting and an opportunity to ask questions and discuss difficulties. Many students don't approach tutors until they are way behind in their work, so receive low grades or even fail a piece of work.

Reassure your teenager that it is common for tertiary students to initially receive *lower* marks than those achieved at school. Encourage them to make appointments to consult academic staff (most welcome questions from students) and to be patient. There are thousands of students in tertiary institutions and it takes *time* to make appointments and find people. Explain that examples of tertiary-level essays are also available from Student Services, institution libraries or on-campus websites.

Persistence/determination

Many students are initially overwhelmed by the lack of boundaries, rules and guidelines common in most high schools.

Show you are aware of the enormous differences between high school and tertiary life. Encourage your teenager to 'hang in there' and give themselves *time to find their feet*. Teenagers who know their parents are realistic and understanding are often more willing to share their concerns.

A successful tertiary student:

- knows how to build up a new friendship support base;
- is self-reliant;
- is self-disciplined—will occasionally say 'no' to the million and one parties;
- is well-informed—knows where to get help on campus and is confident enough to ask for it;
- knows their parents don't have unrealistic expectations;
- knows they can tell parents if they are unhappy in their course;
- knows their parents will support them through this adjustment period;
- knows it's possible to change direction once they enter tertiary study.

FAQs

Q: I've heard that many students start their courses and become disillusioned with their choice. What should parents do if this happens?

A: Many first-year courses do tend to cover basic ground and so may not be as exciting as imagined. Make sure your teenager knows this and encourage them to stick at it for at least a semester unless they are certain the course doesn't suit them. The biggest mistake many make is not telling anyone how they feel. They stop going to classes and eventually fall so far behind they fail. Ideally students should talk to parents, course advisers and counsellors at their institution if they are unhappy with their course or having any difficulties adjusting to tertiary life. This may help them resolve issues and settle into their current course or identify a better course. It's not unusual for students to transfer into other courses.

Q: How can I tell if my teenager is adjusting well to tertiary studies?
A: Some teenagers will be more willing to chat than others and you may have to watch for tell-tale signs that all is not well, such as:
◎ uncharacteristic changes in mood, sleeping or eating patterns;
◎ evasive answers or a sudden unwillingness to discuss studies;
◎ over-insistence that everything is *fine*;
◎ overdoing the parties or withdrawing from friends/family/interests—both are danger signs;
◎ part-time work encroaching on study time and time to establish a friendship base.

> **Professor Craig McInnis, director, Centre for the Study of Higher Education, University of Melbourne**
>
> Undergraduates now work an average of fifteen hours per week; 40 per cent work sixteen hours or more and 18 per cent work 21 hours or more. Having to balance full-time study with part-time work, universities are no longer the place to meet friends for life. A substantial number will go through university without making any friends at all.

Common myths preventing a smooth transition to tertiary studies

Myth 1: 'Uni is easy after high school!'

Many students going into tertiary study are shocked by the enormous demands of their courses. Believing that it's all supposed to be easy can make studies disillusioning and lead to real self-doubt. 'Everyone else seems to be coping except me.'

Hannah, 20

Everyone tells you uni is a pushover compared to school. *It'll be crazy. Lots of alcohol and party, party, party!'* But it's not true. You do have to work hard and it's not easy. Eighty per cent of my friends dropped out during their first year. I made it through but it was a shock to find everything was different to the picture you're given.

What can parents do?

While it's important to celebrate your teenager's move into tertiary studies, encourage them to talk to students who have successfully completed first-year studies. This helps them to form a realistic picture of what is expected in their course. Encourage them to attend Orientation Week at their new institution, where they can speak to current students. While reassuring them that you believe they have the ability and discipline required to pass, point out that no tertiary course is a 'pushover'. Teenagers should know it's okay to say they find the going tough—that this is the norm, not the exception. 'Tertiary study is hard. You don't have to excel at everything. Give yourself a break and enjoy studies a bit more. Give yourself time to adjust and get into the swing of things.'

Myth 2: 'No one cares about you at uni or TAFE. You sink or swim!'

While tertiary environments are much larger and more impersonal than high school, students need to know that they are *not* simply a number at university and TAFE. *The perception that no one cares is very dangerous.* It often prevents students from seeking support, thus ensuring that they do indeed fall on their faces.[6]

What can parents do?

Ensure your teenager is familiar with all the support services available at university and TAFE. Tell them that seeking some assistance in adjusting to tertiary life is *common*.

If you don't believe the transition can be difficult, listen to these stories . . .

Nadia, 22

I dropped out of uni because I didn't like my course and didn't know what to do. I didn't know who to talk to and who to go to. That was two years ago but my parents still think I'm at uni. At the start, I used to get up every day and leave the house so they would think I was still at uni. I had no job and nothing to do. Eventually I found a job and had somewhere to go each day. I can't tell mum and dad about uni because I'm scared of hurting them and scared of their reaction. They're good parents. They love me . . . I know that.

I feel like a thief in my own house—like I'm stealing something from them by not telling them the truth. I feel like a stranger. Sometimes I think I'm going to fall apart. I haven't had a good night's sleep in a long, long time.

Nadia's 19-year-old sister Joanne was the only person who knew she had left university. The experience of not feeling able to be honest with their parents pushed these young people to breaking point. Joanne felt she was caught between betraying her parents and not wanting to betray her sister. 'I just want this to end.' Both cried as they spoke to me of being unable to sleep well and living in constant fear of the truth being discovered. Their fear of disappointing loving parents was preventing them from being honest.

After much reassurance, these young people found the courage to finally tell their parents the truth. Ironically, they had guessed that something was amiss and were waiting for Nadia to approach them. Although shocked at hearing what had happened, they were delighted to have their daughters 'back'.

Dr Barry Rogers, university chaplain and psychologist

Students should know what support staff are available at university. Many take ages to approach us and only find out through word of mouth. 'I went to a counsellor. They're not too bad.' Many students have difficulty making connections at university and start skipping classes when they don't know anyone in their lecture. Those who go to activities in Orientation Week and get involved in the social side of university have a better chance of surviving.

I can only imagine the stress these sisters endured over the two-year period. Both recently told me how wonderful it is to be able to sleep again without worrying about what might happen the next day. This is not the first time I have encountered situations like this. Many students are afraid to tell their families they are lonely at university, feel unhappy about their courses or are struggling to pass. It's hard to admit you are struggling at the very point in your life when you are supposed to be more independent.

Recently a distraught parent phoned me. The previous evening her son had burst into tears, revealing he had failed *everything* in his second semester at university. 'He's devastated and so are we. You know what upset us the most? That he couldn't come to us when he started having problems. He was afraid to tell us. We can't get over that . . . our own son afraid to talk to us. And you know what he said? "What's going to happen to me?" He's so frightened. We thought he was okay. We thought he would tell us if anything went wrong.'

What's concerning is that these parents have a great relationship with their son. So what went wrong? Ironically, part of the problem is that this student had always passed everything at school and had never experienced much difficulty with studies. When 'Tony' started floundering at university, he didn't know how to bring up the subject and once again was scared of disappointing loving parents who had always been so proud of him. Having always been a successful student, Tony also didn't know how to cope when studies became difficult. He also had not considered asking for help from support staff at university.

I've seen many students in this situation. Perhaps we should pre-empt these situations and talk to young people about the highs and lows in life—*especially those who have had a dream run*. At some point everyone comes a cropper. That's life! Your teenager may need to hear you say this. This opens the possibility that they can approach you knowing that you won't be shocked or disappointed if they do find the going hard.

Support available to help students survive the tertiary study blues

- Academic advisers will help with areas like administration, enrolling, choosing subjects and organising tutorials.
- Tutors and lecturers have consultation times.
- Learning Skills Centres offer help with areas such as taking good lecture notes, working out a study timetable, writing

tertiary-level essays, exams, oral presentations, and other skills needed for academic success.
◎ Health and medical services.
◎ Confidential counselling.
◎ Chaplains for personal and spiritual support and counselling.
◎ Child care.
◎ Financial help and advice.
◎ Accommodation.
◎ Careers and employment advice.
◎ Legal advice.

Employment blues

Finding employment and starting full-time work are major milestones for anyone. It is an exhilarating experience for some teenagers, but research shows that many—even those who previously worked part-time—are initially nervous about starting work. Many describe the first day as a 'frightening experience'.[7] One recent report found that 43 per cent of early school leavers and 19 per cent of school completers experienced a troubled transition.[8]

Sophie Evans, 23, youth employment officer

I would like to say my journey from university to the workforce was smooth and stress-free, but it wasn't. I did a Social Science degree at university and had an absolute ball. With new friends, pub-crawls and late night exam studying, the three years flew by. Before I knew it, I was out in the real world and had to get a job. Not a job—*a career*. That's even scarier.

I felt like I had been dancing in a nightclub when suddenly someone turns the lights on and pushes me on stage, and I'm standing there not knowing what to do. I didn't even know what I could do with my degree. And I panicked. Over a three-month period I visited my careers teacher at university over six times. I needed her to look over my résumé, tell me if my answers to her practice interview questions were correct, and to basically reassure me that I would be fine.

I settled into a daily routine of getting up at 9.00 a.m., printing out possible jobs on employment websites, and cutting out vacancies from various papers. I would then paste these into my scrapbook and sit there examining, scrutinising and over-analysing whether I was good enough to apply. I would probably apply for one in every six. I was scared in case I wasn't good enough and they would scoff at my lack of experience. I was scared because what if they liked me and wanted an interview!

While my family was supportive, I felt very alone during this time. For the first time in my life, it seemed everything was up to me. I didn't share my feelings because I didn't want anyone to know how scared I was and I didn't want to look like I couldn't handle things.

Attending interview after interview did nothing for my confidence. I became disheartened and frustrated. During this time, mum managed to break my shell. She sat with me and discussed how I felt and what my next move would be. Her support and encouragement enabled me to put things into perspective and also lifted some of the responsibility and burden that I had been carrying alone for so long.

Looking back, I should have utilised my family's support more and not isolated myself into this bottle of fear, stress and panic. I should also have had more confidence in my own ability.

Because many teenagers are reluctant to reveal their concerns, once your teenager finds work, it's important to make sure they are adjusting well. Is the boss approachable? What are their co-workers like? Does the workplace have a relaxed atmosphere or are workers generally stressed? Share some of your own experiences of starting work and reassure your teenager that it sometimes takes a little time to adjust to a workplace. It's also important to reassure them that in the future they can always return to full- or part-time study if they wish. This is particularly important for teenagers who have had negative experiences at high school and for those whose results are not as good as they expected. The most important message is that they have endless options and you will support them, *whatever they decide.*

Some teenagers find work a huge let-down after years of study. I've seen many students in their first jobs after graduating from high school, a TAFE course or even university, asking me: 'This is it? I thought work would be so much better than school!' Sometimes, parents need to ground their first-job expectations. No one starts out as the hotel manager straight out of a hospitality course . . . unless you're a Hilton!

Whatever the reaction, tell your teenager that they don't have to be in love with their first job. If things don't work out as expected, they can find another job, go back to study or even work part-time while completing other courses. Sometimes teenagers are unhappy in their first full-time job because they are in the wrong career area or an unsuitable work environment. Finding out you *don't* like a field of study or a job after all is a useful learning experience, however. You can help them investigate alternative career areas and workplaces.

Teenagers must know that there are no brick walls. It might prevent a few from hitting one! They can always change career direction, retrain, go back to study or have 'time out' to think about various options. 'I feel like the clock's ticking' a recent university graduate told me! This student was under the impression that he would miss out on something if he didn't continually look over his shoulder. This is a heavy burden for a young person to carry. Somehow we have to inject back more of an 'enjoy the ride' outlook.

Sophie Evans, 23, youth employment officer

My work involves helping young people find employment and it's clear that the transition from school to work is often under-estimated. I have witnessed teachers who slap an address in the student's hand and wish them good luck. For some this is fine. But for most, it's not. Students need support from friends and teachers, but more importantly from their parents. When I first began this position I rarely questioned students on how they were feeling about leaving school. Most made out they knew what they were doing and what to expect. They wanted to appear in control—but pretending only goes so far.

Two of the first questions I now ask students who are entering the workforce are: 'Do you feel work ready?' and, 'Are you scared?' I must admit that I have been surprised by the number of teenagers who admit they are scared, particularly the 'cool' guys who are going into apprenticeships or full-time work. The main concerns I hear are: 'What if I don't like the job?' 'What if I don't fit in?' 'What if I'm not good enough?' and 'What if something goes wrong?'

Often teenagers won't let their parents know how they feel because, as we all know, that's not cool. They put up a front, and act like they are fine and don't need any help. As a result, parents are left feeling uncertain about the teenager's transition and also their role as a parent in that transition.

Finding their place in the world

Many teenagers are in no-man's land as they enter the world beyond school. They dance backwards and forwards—one moment the child you knew, the next an unfamiliar young adult. And this can continue for a number of years as young people find their feet and gain confidence.

Anna Masters, 20

I live with my parents, although the thought of moving out occasionally crosses my mind because the space and freedom would be ideal. Numerous times I have threatened to move out after an argument with a parent or sibling. It sounds ridiculous to 'threaten' to move out because I am old enough to do so of my own free will and, as my mum pointed out to me, I only stay because it is convenient for me, which is partly true.

My parents are great, but sometimes I wish that they would back off a little so I could find my feet. I have a friend who moved to the city, and she has to attend to everything. I look at her and wonder if I would be able to live independently because I am so used to someone else worrying about the bills and grocery shopping. During high school I never considered getting a job. It wasn't until afterwards that it became necessary. It took me a while to build the confidence and experience to hold a permanent job. I was never good at budgeting my money, and before I knew it, it was all gone. Now that I'm 20, a full-time student and thinking about travelling, I wish I had saved some of it.

Some people my age are already working full-time, travelling, or renting. I met a girl who married last year at the age of 19 and another girl who lives in a house with five others, is on the dole with no prospects of study or a career, and recently had a baby. I am overwhelmed by these events because I could never see myself in that position. For me, 20 is still too young to make those sorts of decisions, particularly when so many of us don't know what courses to choose, let alone making lifetime decisions.

What I worry most about being 20 is that I am 'coming of age' quicker than I am ready to. Sometimes I still feel 17, naïve and confused.

These are the years when your teenager is testing those wings you have helped them to strengthen. They are also the years when teenagers begin to realise that with the new freedoms come hefty responsibilities. Coming back to that fishing analogy—judge carefully when to give them distance and when they need you close by, when to ask and when to stay silent. Accept the decisions they make and the paths they take even when they are not the ones you would have them take.

Stepping out of school isn't the end of a young person's education—life's education is only beginning. Life will inevitably throw them a few curve balls. This is where you come in. Make sure your teenager knows that, even as their world continues to change, your love and support will remain their constant.

There are few things more uplifting than seeing a young person looking and feeling *on top of the world.* Some take no time to tap into the amazing energy that comes with youth; others meander their way until one day everything falls into place. Parents can help enormously by being open to and accepting of the many exciting educational, career, personal and life pathways open to young people. Encourage them to take the road less travelled.

We all want encouragement and support from people who matter the most—our parents and family. 'I'm proud of you. Look how far you've come. Your whole life is ahead of you.' For a young person embarking on a new phase in life, these words are indelibly life-affirming. These are the words they will carry with them for the rest of their lives. Make them words that will uplift them and encourage them to step forward in life and find their own place in this world.

Though it's difficult to not instinctively reach out and want to protect your teenager, let them go. Trust that the words, values and self-belief you have given them will stay with them as they ride the highs and lows of life ahead.

There are only two lasting bequests we can hope to give our children. One of these is roots, the other, wings.
—Hodding Carter

Final thoughts . . .
Passing the baton

As a rule, I detest reality TV but found myself hooked on *Frontier House*, the American program where three families were transported back in time to 1883. As far as possible, the families lived as frontier pioneers. They built their own homes, and raised crops and animals. I was fascinated with how their teenagers reacted to all of this. While there were fights, tensions and tantrums, the transformation that eventually occurred in these young people was remarkable. By the end of the experiment they had grown to love working side by side with their parents. Sure it was hard and confronting and lacking in all of the creature comforts teenagers adore, but it was rewarding and challenging. There were obstacles to be faced and conquered every day. These teenagers were given responsibilities that most parents today wouldn't even dream of giving their children. Did they measure up? You bet!

Trust, responsibility, challenge. These are the things lacking in the lives of so many teenagers today who feel directionless, disillusioned and detached from life. These are the things that you can nurture in your teenager as they journey through high school. The young people in the frontier experiment were given opportunities to learn that they had far greater resources, talents and resilience than they had ever imagined possible. 'I've discovered imagination,' the younger boy, Logan, said. One of the older teenagers stated that she no longer cared so much about what people thought of her. 'I've learnt confidence in who I am and what I am.' Give your teenager the opportunity to be imaginative and creative. Don't just *give*.

Short of going bush, how can you help your teenager reach the level of self-confidence and self-acceptance these 'frontier teenagers' displayed? Give them opportunities to learn to trust themselves, to find their undiscovered abilities, to develop strength of character and initiative. Encourage them to seize opportunities that arise both in and out of school. Allow them to take steps and make mistakes, knowing that you will not judge them. Stand back and let them find themselves with the knowledge that, should they need you, you will be there in a heartbeat. *Above all, teach them that they have the power to recreate themselves and to become whoever and whatever they choose.*

If you can achieve these things for your children, you are providing the best education of all. They'll have the confidence and determination needed to be happy in the world beyond those school gates—regardless of scores achieved or pathways chosen. They'll be self-assured and independent young adults capable of standing on their own feet and carving their own unique place in the world. Mission accomplished!

Notes

Introduction

1. Resnick, M.D., Bearman, P., Blum, R. et al., 'Protecting adolescents from harm: Findings from the national longitudinal study on adolescent health', *Journal of the American Medical Association*, vol. 278, no. 10, 1997, pp. 823–32.

Chapter 2

1. Cohen, D., *How to Succeed in Psychometric Tests*, Wrightbooks, Sydney, 2001.
2. Gardner, H., *Multiple Intelligences—The Theory in Practice*, Basic Books, New York, 1993.
   Gardner, H., *Frames of Mind—The Theory of Multiple Intelligences*, Fontana Books, London, 1993.
3. Goleman, D., *Emotional Intelligence—Why It Can Matter More than IQ*, Bantam Books, New York, 1995.
4. Attwood, A., 'The last shall be first and the first can flunk', *The Age*, 19 December 2002.

Chapter 3

1. Meeus, W. and Dekovic, M., 'Identity development and peer support in adolescence: results of a national Dutch survey', *Adolescence*, vol. 30, no. 120, 1995, pp. 931–43.

2. Janus, S.S. and Janus, C.L., *The Janus Report on Sexual Behavior*, Wiley, New York, 1993.
3. Figgis, J., *The Landscape of Support for Youth in Transition*, Department of Education, Science and Training, Canberra, 2004.

Chapter 5

1. Griffin, K.W., Epstein, J.A., Botvin, G.J. and Spoth, R.L., 'Social competence and substance use among rural youth: mediating role of social benefit expectancies of use', *Journal of Youth and Adolescence*, vol. 30, no. 4, August 2001, pp. 485–98.
2. Dunn, A., 'Blues when young could lead to dementia in later life', *The Age*, 4 September 2003.

Chapter 6

1. Dryden, G. and Vos, J., *The Learning Revolution—A Lifelong Learning Programme for the World's Finest Computer: Your Amazing Brain*, Accelerated Learning Systems Ltd, London, 1994.
2. West, Andrew, 'All-boys schools make better men', *The Sun-Herald*, 6 July 2003.

Chapter 7

1. Wang, M.C., Haertel, G.D. and Walberg, H.J., 'Toward a knowledge base for school learning', *Review of Educational Research*, vol. 63, no. 3, 1993, pp. 249–94.
2. Resnick, M.D., Bearman, P., Blum, R. et al., 'Protecting adolescents from harm: Findings from the national longitudinal study on adolescent health', *Journal of the American Medical Association*, vol. 278, no. 10, 1997, pp. 823–32.
3. *Equality of Educational Opportunity Report*, often referred to as the Coleman Report after the principal researcher, Dr James Coleman, Washington, 1966.
4. Finn, J.D., 'Parental engagement that makes a difference', *Educational Leadership*, vol. 55, no. 8, 1998, pp. 20–24.

5. Bryce, J., Frigo, T., McKenzie, P. and Withers, G., *The Era of Lifelong Learning: Implications for Secondary Schools*, Australian Council for Educational Research, Canberra, 2000.

Chapter 8

1. Lindsay, J., Smith, A. and Rosenthal, D., *Secondary Students, HIV/AIDS and Sexual Health*, Centre for the Study of Sexually Transmissible Diseases, La Trobe University, Melbourne, 1998.
2. SIECUS (Sex Information and Education Council of the United States), 'Issues and answers fact sheet on sexuality education', *SIECUS Report*, vol. 27, no. 6, 1999, pp. 29–34, cited in Goldman, J., 'Sexuality education for teenagers in the new millennium', *Youth Studies Australia*, vol. 19, no. 4, December 2000, pp. 11–19.
3. Mitchell, K.J., Finkelhor, D. and Wolak, J., 'The exposure of youth to unwanted sexual material on the internet: A national survey of risk, impact and prevention', *Journal of Youth and Society*, vol. 34, no. 3, 2003, pp. 330–58.
4. Smith, A., Agius, P., Dyson, S., Mitchell, A. and Pitts, M., *Secondary Students and Sexual Health 2002*, Monograph Series No. 47, Australian Research Centre in Sex, Health and Society, La Trobe University, Melbourne, 2003.
5. Smith et al., *Secondary Students and Sexual Health*.
6. Savin-Williams, R.C., *Gay and Lesbian Youth: Expressions of Identity*, Hemisphere Publishing, New York, 1990.
7. Lindsay et al., *Secondary Students, HIV/AIDS and Sexual Health*.
8. Hollander, G., 'Questioning youths: Challenges to working with youths forming identities', *School Psychology Review*, vol. 29, no. 2, 2000, pp. 173–79.
9. D'Augelli, A.R., 'Developmental implications of victimization of lesbian, gay and bisexual youths', in G.M. Herek, (ed.), *Psychological Perspectives on Lesbian and Gay Issues*, vol. 4, 1998, pp. 187–210; and Tharinger, D. and Wells, G., 'An attachment perspective on the developmental challenges of gay and lesbian adolescents: The need for continuity of caregiving from family and schools', *School Psychology Review*, vol. 29, no. 2, 2000, pp. 158–72.
10. Hillier, L. and Walsh, J., 'Abused, silenced and ignored: Creating more supportive environments for same sex attracted young people',

Australian Institute of Family Studies, *Youth Suicide Prevention Bulletin*, no. 3, 1999, pp. 23–27. (The first Australian large scale study undertaken into the well-being of same sex-attracted youth); and Kids Help Line Infosheet No. 20.

11. Rosario, M., Hunter, J. and Gwadz, M., 'Exploration of substance abuse among lesbian, gay and bisexual youth: Prevalence and correlates', *Journal of Adolescent Research*, vol. 12 , no. 4, 1997, pp. 454–76.

12. Savin-Williams, *Gay and Lesbian Youth: Expressions of Identity*, Hemisphere Publishing, USA, 1990.

13. Remafedi, G., French, S., Story, M., Resnick, M. and Blum, R., 'The relationship between suicide risk and sexual orientation: Results of a population based study', *American Journal of Public Health*, vol. 87, no. 8, 1997, pp. 1–4.

14. McCarthy, S.J., 'Home–school connectedness: A review of literature', *Journal of Educational Research*, vol. 93, no. 3, 2000, pp. 145–53.

Chapter 9

1. www.kidshelp.com.au. Infosheets available from this website contain great information for young people and parents.

2. Field, E., *Bullybusting: How to Help Children Deal with Teasing and Bullying*, Finch Publishing, Sydney, 1999.

3. Kids Help Line Infosheet No. 7

4. Field, *Bullybusting*.

5. Kids Help Line Infosheet No. 7.

6. Withers, G. and Russell, J., *Educating for Resilience: Prevention and Intervention Strategies for Young People at Risk*, Catholic Education Office, Melbourne, 1998.

7. Glover, S., Burns, J., Butler, H. and Patton, G., 'Social environments and the emotional well-being of young people', *Family Matters*, vol. 49, Autumn, 1998, pp. 11–15.

8. Roeser, R., Midgley, C. and Urdan, T., 'Perceptions of the school psychological environment and early adolescents: psychological and behavioural functioning in school: The mediating role of goals and belonging', *Journal of Educational Psychology*, vol. 88, no. 3, 1996, pp. 408–22; and Goodenow, C., 'Classroom belonging among early adolescent students: Relationships to motivation and achievement', *Journal of Early Adolescence*, vol. 13, no. 1, 1993, pp. 21–43.

9. Polesel, J., Helme, S., Davies, M., Teese, R., Nicholas, T. and Vickers, M., *VET in Schools: Culture, Policy and the Employment and Training Impact*, National Centre for Vocational Education Research, Canberra, 2002.

10. Knight, B. A. and Becker, T., 'The challenge of meeting the needs of gifted students in the regular classroom: The student viewpoint', *The Australasian Journal of Gifted Education*, vol. 9, no. 1, 2000, pp. 11–17.

11. Long, M. and Dusseldorp Skills Forum, *How Young People are Faring 2004*, Dusseldorp Skills Forum, Sydney, 2004.

12. Lee, V.E. and Burkham, D.T., 'Dropping out of high school: The role of school organization and structure', *American Educational Research Journal*, vol. 40, no. 2, Summer 2003, pp. 353–93.

13. Hargreaves, A., Earl, L. and Ryan, J., *Schooling for Change: Re-inventing Schools for Early Adolescents*, Falmer Press, London, 1996, Ch. 5.

Chapter 10

1. Levy, S. and Murray, J., 'Demystifying tertiary success: Strategies for broadening participation and initiating lifelong learning', *The Journal of the Institute for Access Studies and The European Access Network*, vol. 5, no. 2, 2003, pp. 42–45.

2. Wolfe, P., *Brain Matters: Translating Research into Classroom Practice*, ASCD, Alexandria, VA, USA, 2001.

3. Eckersley, R., 'Values and visions: Youth and the failure of modern Western culture', *Youth Studies Australia*, Autumn, vol. 14, 1995, pp. 13–21; and Hicks, D., 'A lesson for the future: Young people's hopes and fears for tomorrow', *Futures*, vol. 28, no. 1, 1996, pp. 1–13.

4. Gidley, J.M., 'An intervention targeting hopelessness in adolescents by promoting positive future images', *Australian Journal of Guidance and Counselling*, vol. 11, no. 1, 2001, pp. 51–64.

5. Horsefield, P., 'Church and the electronic culture', in P. Ballis and G. Bouma (eds), *Religion in an Age of Reason*, Christian Research Association, Melbourne, 1999, pp. 137–53.

6. Zbar, V., Brown, D. and Bereznicki, B., The *Values Education Study, Final Report, 2003*, Curriculum Corporation, Melbourne, 2003.

Chapter 12

1. Helme, S. and Polesel, J., *Young Visions 2003: A Follow-up Study of Young Visions Participants and Their Destinations One Year Later*, Department of Education, Science and Training, Australia, 2004.
2. Maiden, S., 'Uni students' first-year blues', *The Australian*, 15 December 2003.
3. Rood, D., 'Twenty-two per cent quit study at Deakin', *The Age*, 16 June 2004.
4. Kantanis, T., 'The role of social transition in students' adjustment to the first year of university', *Journal of Institutional Research*, vol. 9, no. 1, 2000, pp. 100–110.
5. Kantanis, 'The role of social transition'.
6. Peel, M., 'Nobody cares: The challenge of isolation in school to university transition', *Journal of Institutional Research*, vol. 9, no. 1, 2003, pp. 22–34.
7. Smith, E., 'The first job: Experiences of young Australians starting full-time work', *Youth Studies Australia*, vol. 22, no. 1, 2003, pp. 11–17.
8. Long, M. and Dusseldorp Skills Forum, *How Young People are Faring 2004*, Dusseldorp Skills Forum, Sydney 2004.

Recommended reading

Carr-Gregg, M. and Shale, E., *Adolescence: A Guide for Parents*, Finch Publishing, Sydney, 2002, Ch. 9. Information on teenage depression, youth suicide, eating disorders and drugs.

Donaghy, B., *Anna's Story*, Angus & Robertson, Sydney, 1996. A must-read if you believe your teenager might be experimenting with drugs. It offers real insight into issues affecting teenagers and would be a great starting point for conversation around this topic.

Lashley, C. and Best, W., *12 Steps to Study Success*, Continuum Press, New York, 2001. (Contains information on organising a study timetable, improving reading skills, research and essay writing.)

Lightfoot, C., *The Culture of Adolescent Risk-taking*, Guildford Press, New York, 1997.

Ponton, L.E., *The Romance of Risk: Why Teenagers Do the Things They Do*, Basic Books, New York, 1997.

Shale, E., *The Complete Survival Guide for High School and Beyond*, Harper-Collins, Melbourne, 2004. (Motivates teenagers to enjoy school and achieve their best. It gives them practical suggestions on improving study and exam techniques, memory, time management, goal-setting and other skills required to increase their enjoyment of school.)

Shale, E. (ed.) *Inside Out: An Australian Collection of Coming Out Stories*, Bookman Press, Melbourne, 1999. These are autobiographical stories from Australians of all ages but mainly from young people. Stories give insights into issues confronting young people in their journey towards self-acceptance.

Teenage fiction—centred around teenagers questioning their sexuality.

Hines, S., *Out of the Shadows*, Random House, Sydney, 1998.

Pausacker, J., *What Are Ya?*, Angus & Robinson, Sydney, 1998.

Walker, S., *The Year of Freaking Out*, Pan Macmillan, Sydney, 1997.

Walker, S., *Peter*, Omnibus Books, Sydney, 1991.

Although these novels are written for teenagers, they also offer adults great insights into the issues confronting young people who question their sexuality or who identify themselves as gay.

Support services

Contact nationally recognised support services in your area. These provide excellent information for parents and teenagers on all drugs and drug prevention disorders and sexuality. Most support services also have excellent websites. Always ensure that you only access websites established by reputable organisations. For issues surrounding sexuality, P–FLAG (Parents and Friends of Gays and Lesbians) offers excellent advice and support. www.psy.mq.edu.au/MUARU is a great website where programs and resources available for anxious children and teenagers can be found. Access other reputable websites and organisations in your area. Most support services have very informative fact sheets for parents and teenagers.

On bullying and anxiety

Atwood, M., *Cat's Eye*, Virago Press, London, 1990. Although fiction, this offers one of the most revealing insights into the effects of bullying on young people. A must-read if you believe your teenager has or is being bullied.

Field, E., *Bullybusting: How to Help Children Deal with Teasing and Bullying*, Finch Publishing, Sydney, 1999.

Rapee, R.M., Wignall, A., Hudson, J.L. and Schniering, C.A., *Treating Anxious Children and Adolescents: An Evidence-based Approach*, New Harbinger Publications, Oakland, CA, 2000.

Rapee, R.M. (ed.) *Helping your Anxious child: A Step-by-step Guide for Parents*, New Harbinger Publications, Oakland, CA, 2000.

Simmons, R., *Odd Girl Out: The Hidden Culture of Aggression in Girls*, Blackinc Books, Melbourne, 2002. This book offers real-life case studies and fascinating insights into the effects of bullying. It would be great reading for teenagers, as it reinforces the fact that victims of bullying are not to blame and outlines the great relief victims experience at talking about what is happening.

Index